Pha

Phantom
MICHAEL
CRAWFORD
Unmasked

ANTHONY HAYWARD

WEIDENFELD AND NICOLSON
LONDON

Published in Great Britain by
George Weidenfeld & Nicolson Limited
91 Clapham High Street
London SW4 7TA

This paperback edition published by
George Weidenfeld & Nicolson Limited 1992

ISBN 0 297 81243 2

Printed in Great Britain by
The Guernsey Press Co. Ltd, Guernsey, Channel Islands

CONTENTS

ILLUSTRATIONS

With Michele Dotrice in *Some Mothers Do 'Ave 'Em* (BBC)

In a window-cleaning stunt for *Some Mothers Do 'Ave 'Em* (Syndication International)

Another terrifying stunt – Crawford as a motorcycle courier (BBC)

Crawford's first starring role in *Billy* (Zoe Dominic)

With co-star Cheryl Kennedy (Associated Newspapers)

With Barbara Carrera in *Condorman* (Walt Disney)

Crawford sings, juggles and treads the high wire in his role as Barnum (Press Association)

With Sarah Brightman in *The Phantom of the Opera* (Clive Barda)

ACKNOWLEDGEMENTS

For general help in researching this book, I wish to thank the British Film Institute Library; the Theatre Museum, Covent Garden, London; and the British Newspaper Library. For special help in areas of specific research, I am grateful to the staff of the Britten-Pears Library, Aldeburgh, Suffolk; the Children's Film & Television Foundation; the Belgrade Theatre, Coventry; the Central Library, Coventry; the Nottingham Playhouse; the County Library, Nottingham; the Ministry of Defence Air Historical Branch; the Public Record Office; and the Register of Births, Marriages & Deaths.

For their reminiscences, I would like to thank Raymond Allen, Alan Benson, Gavin Birkett, Marc Boyle, Bernard Braden, Jeremy Bulloch, Patsy Byrne, Roy Castle, James Cossins, Peter Dobereiner, Stuart Fell, Rick Gauld, Melvyn Hayes, Colin Graham, Charles Jarrott, Freddie Jones, Richard Lester, Innes Lloyd, Leo McKern, Ken McReddie, Ronald Magill, Stephen Moore, Terence Morgan, Val Musetti, Ronald Neame, Alvin Rakoff, Oliver Reed, James Roose-Evans, Alan Rothwell, Peter Graham Scott, Ned Sherrin, Derek Ware, David Watkin and Claude Whatham. Special thanks are due to film critic Alan Frank, an unending source of help and advice. Photographic credits are included in the List of Illustrations. Excerpts from previously published material are credited in the notes at the back of the book.

Anthony Hayward

Chapter 1

THE LITTLE SWEEP

Mesmerized by the bewitching performance of Danny Kaye at the Lewisham Metropolitan, and thrilling to the spectacle of Bertram Mills' Circus, the young Michael Crawford dreamed of entering this world of fantasy. Many years later, starring in the musical *Barnum*, he would be walking the high wire, juggling and riding the unicycle himself, and breaking Danny Kaye's record number of appearances at the London Palladium. Showbusiness gave the youngster a chance to escape into another world, away from the frustrations of an unsettled childhood.

Asked in interviews about his parents, Crawford tells the story of his RAF sergeant-pilot father who was shot down and killed during the Second World War, before his birth. Whether he knew it or not, the truth was slightly different. Sgt Arthur Dumbell Smith married Doris Pike on the Isle of Sheppey, in Kent, on 27 August 1939[1]. As a Spitfire pilot in the Battle of Britain, he was shot down over Ashford, Kent, on 4 September 1940 and died two days later[2], sixteen months before the birth of his wife Doris's son, Michael.

Doris had been born in Southampton[3], but her parents, Montague and Edith Pike, later moved to Minster, on Sheppey. At the age of eighteen, Doris was turning heads on the island and was selected as Sheerness Carnival Queen from fifteen entrants; one of the judges was Frank Forbes-Robertson, a film star of the time.

Exactly a week after Doris wed Sgt Smith, at Sheerness Catholic Church, Britain declared war on Germany. The couple were both twenty-one and, after the wedding, had gone to live in Cambridgeshire, where Sgt Smith, in the RAF's 66 Squadron, was based.

1

By this time, 66 Squadron was fully equipped with Spitfires[4] at Duxford, ready to play a major role in defending Britain when the *Luftwaffe* struck. Sgt Smith was involved in many test flights during those early days of the war, before patrolling over the North Sea[5]. In February 1940, Flying Officer Douglas Bader, who had lost his legs in a flying accident nine years earlier and was discharged from the RAF, rejoined and was posted to Duxford, and soon became a celebrated officer in Fighter Command, complete with tin legs, although he ended the war in Colditz[6].

When the British evacuation of Dunkirk came in May and June 1940, Sgt Smith was one of those pilots who gave air cover to the boats ferrying Servicemen back from France[7]. At about this time, 66 Squadron moved from Duxford to a new aerodrome at Coltishall, in Norfolk. By July, the Germans had swept through Belgium, the Netherlands and France, and the Battle of Britain was under way, with the *Luftwaffe* flying across Kent and East Anglia in an attempt to reach London and other major cities.

On 9 July, Sgt Smith and a colleague were in a dogfight with an enemy aircraft over the North Sea, south-east of Great Yarmouth. None of the pilots was killed, but Sgt Smith recorded the event in a Combat Report:

Sent up approx 16.10 hrs to patrol base at 18000 [feet]. Enemy sighted over St Faiths at 1625 hrs by Red 2 who noticed a streak of black smoke. At that time we were at 11000 and E/A [enemy aircraft] at 17000. E/A turned and made off East at the same time as we sighted him. We gave chase using extra boost and climbing to height of 16000. E/A kept on steady course at about 220mph until attacked, when he dived down to sea level at about 250–280pmh [sic] and I made two attacks one at 16000 when E/A took slight evasive action by executing gentle turns. It was after this attack that he commenced to dive (Red 2 then carried out at [sic] attack). During my first attack I experienced some very inaccurate return fire which ceased just before I broke away. Red 2 experienced no return fire, on either of his attacks, and I experienced none on my second attack, during which I closed range to 100 yds and concentrated on engines of E/A with no visible effect. Engagement terminated through lack of ammunition.[8]

Fifteen days later, while on convoy patrol over the North Sea, Sgt Smith was in another air fight. Suddenly smoke and oil poured from his Spitfire, which was in danger of crashing. Fortunately he managed to make a 'pancake' landing on the water and, after two minutes in the sea, was rescued by a destroyer[9]. He was badly shaken and needed nine stitches in a head injury. Sgt Smith was granted leave, during which he returned to Sheppey[10].

September 1940 was a critical month for Britain as the *Luftwaffe* stepped up its attacks. On the fourth, a day after 66 Squadron moved from Coltishall to Kenley, in Surrey, there was a morning of all-out German attacks on Kent airfields. It was one of the worst days for RAF casualties. At 10am, Sgt Smith was shot down while in combat with a German fighter over Ashford and crashed at Chequer Tree Farm, Mersham[11]. He baled out before his burning plane crashed; only fragments of it have been found. Locals recalled a pilot parachuting into a field behind the farmhouse, with flames coming from his body. Someone rushed out with wet towels to wrap around him[12]. Sgt Smith, seriously wounded, was taken to a casualty clearing station at Benenden, and died two days later[13]. He was buried in the graveyard at St Luke's Church, Whyteleafe, in Airmen's Corner, a plot set aside for those who served at the nearby Kenley base and at Croydon[14]. His headstone, which included his RAF number, reads simply, '580153 Sergeant A D Smith, Pilot, Royal Air Force, 6th September 1940.'[15] His death was reported in the *Sheerness Times & Guardian*:

YOUNG R.A.F. PILOT
KILLED IN ACTION

MARRIED FORMER
SHEERNESS
CARNIVAL QUEEN

A YOUNG flying ace of a Spitfire squadron which has been engaged in many battles over Britain, and who married a former Sheerness Carnival Queen, has been killed in action.

His wife received the official notification from the Air Ministry a few days after they had celebrated their first anniversary of their wedding.

The young pilot was Sergeant-Pilot Arthur Dunbell [*sic*] Smith, only son of Mrs Blake, of London, and the late Major Dunbell [*sic*] Smith. He was only 22 years of age. A little over a year ago he married Miss Doris Pike, daughter of Mr and Mrs M. Pike, of 6, The Crescent, Halfway. She was chosen Carnival Queen of Sheerness in 1936. They were married at the Catholic Church, Sheerness.

Quite recently Sergt.-Pilot Dunbell [*sic*] Smith visited Halfway while on leave. He had been in an air fight, and was compelled to make a 'pancake' landing in the North Sea, in the course of which he was injured. He was rescued by a British destroyer.

It is understood that a few days before his death the young airman shot down a Dornier bomber.

He was buried with full Royal Air Force honours on Wednesday.

There were no wreaths, as it was the wish of the pilot that donations should be sent to the Spitfire Fund.[16]

By the time Sgt Smith's widow, Doris, gave birth to a son, she had been evacuated to Bulford Army camp, on Salisbury Plain, in Wiltshire[17], a large, bleak area of chalk downland. Bulford, where the Avon and the Nine Mile River meet, is just a short distance from Stonehenge, and was one of the first sites on Salisbury Plain to be bought by the War Office at the turn of the century and turned into a garrison, bringing new industry to a village that had previously been dependent on agriculture[18].

Michael Patrick Smith was born illegitimately in the maternity ward of Salisbury Infirmary on 19 January 1942[19]. He and his mother spent the rest of the war at Bulford camp. Apart from a cinema, there were no real forms of entertainment[20]; mixing with Servicemen's wives would have been one of the few ways of passing the days. When peace came in 1945, they moved to Kent, to live with Doris's mother on the Isle of Sheppey. Michael Smith's maternal grandmother was to become an important part of his life many years later, but this stay was cut short by his mother's decision to marry again. On 23 September 1945, at the same church in which she had wed six years earlier, Doris married Lionel Ingram, a grocery store manager who had been an Army sergeant and whose father was an Admiralty official[21].

This meant the first change of name for the young Michael Smith; he became known as Ingram, and there was no love lost between him and his stepfather. The family lived in the Kent town of Bexleyheath before moving to Herne Hill, South London. He went first to a choir school, St Michael's College, Bexley, then, having failed his Eleven-Plus, to Oakfield School, Dulwich, where he received the private education on which his parents were so keen, although that meant sacrifices for them, such as giving up smoking. The youngster never enjoyed school but captained the football team, preferring sport to academic lessons. In class he would play the clown and have the other boys in stitches, but a teacher would walk in and all fingers would point to him. Crawford later recalled, 'I didn't enjoy my last three years at school. I failed the Eleven-Plus – that horrible thing – and that made me feel I wasn't any good. The school was against me. Authority hates a clown; it feels threatened. But, when teachers were nice to me, I worked very hard.'[22]

His escape was singing and acting. He was a choirboy at St Paul's Cathedral, where he had his first starring role, leading a processional, picked to do so, he believed, 'because I looked such a cherub'[23]. Nerves were a problem he always found difficult to combat and the full glare of the spotlight made walking *and* singing a tall order that day. 'I would just mime the words,' he said[24].

At the age of eleven, Michael Ingram made his stage debut in a school production of Benjamin Britten's *Let's Make an Opera* at Brixton Town Hall. Playing the Little Sweep, his clothes were to be ripped off one by one by the Big Sweep and Assistant Sweep – played by the headmaster and French master – as they sang three verses, and then he was to be thrown up the chimney.

On the night, the young soprano was so nervous that he made a fatal mistake: he forgot to put on any underwear. His jacket was torn off during the first verse and his shirt during the second, then the Little Sweep realized he had made a monumental error and tried to tell the two schoolmasters not to remove his trousers. The head thought the young upstart was simply trying to put him off and clouted him, before ripping off his trousers to reveal a naked behind to an audience that included the mayor, and parents and children of the school. His mother was sitting proudly in the fourth row, wearing a silver lamé dress.

Girls cheered and threw money on to the stage, but the curtain came down, the head hit him again and, with the curtain back up, the youngster was caned in the middle of the performance. However, the memory is a happy one. 'That's the day I discovered comedy,' he said[25]. 'It was so wonderful making people laugh, I didn't even feel the thrashing. The relationship that existed between the audience and the cast was unlike anything I had ever experienced.'[26]

Showbusiness had taken its hold; visits to the cinema and theatre convinced the youngster that this was where his future lay. During his teens, the newly emerging rock 'n' roll also influenced him, his favourite singers being Bill Haley, Elvis Presley, Gene Vincent, Pat Boone and Frank Sinatra, but his No 1 was Buddy Holly, who had hits with songs such as 'Peggy Sue' but died at the age of twenty in a plane crash. Big-band music, especially Duke Ellington, and both traditional and modern jazz also appealed to the teenager.

His big break came when a neighbour in Herne Hill pointed out an advertisement in the *Daily Telegraph*; the English Opera Group wanted a boy soprano to star in Benjamin Britten's opera *The Turn of the Screw*. Britten was particularly revered for his vocal scores for children, which captured their imagination and interest without condescension. In 1947 he had formed the English Opera Group, which performed his works[27]. Securing an audition for *The Turn of the Screw*, Michael Ingram recited a poem and sang 'Early One Morning'. In competition with 800 other boys, he made it to the last five, but nerves got the better of him during a final audition at the Criterion Theatre, in London's West End. The role went to David Hemmings, who was to become a film star and, later, a director.

When, six months later, the English Opera Group was looking for a boy soprano to play the Little Sweep in a new production of *Let's Make an Opera*[28] – in which the young Michael Ingram had previously treated a Brixton audience to on-stage nudity – Benjamin Britten remembered Michael, not so much for his singing, but for the havoc he caused at the earlier auditions. This time, the final audition was at Britten's London home, in Regent's Park, and the thirteen-year-old landed the role, which he shared with David Hemmings. 'He [Britten] thought I was too funny to leave out,' Crawford reflected later[29]. 'Perhaps he thought I'd make the rehearsals lively. Certainly, nobody else wanted me, but he said I had character.'

In fact, the teenager's potential was also spotted by Colin Graham, who was assistant producer for the first performances during a short season at the old Scala Theatre, before taking over as producer for a three-month countrywide tour, finishing at London's prestigious Royal Court Theatre. 'The thing that struck one about him was the fantastic charisma and this bright-eyed determination, which he has maintained to this very day,' recalled Graham[30]. 'He was particularly bright and naughty, in a way that you could never really find fault with because he was always so engaging. He and David Hemmings got on very well and got up to a lot of mischievous things. Even then, Michael had this attention to detail and a determination to get everything right and everything around him right. This is something he has carried in a big way into his later professional life. His performance was wonderful. We knew then that he was an absolutely first-class actor and that was going to be his profession. You don't run across these people at that age all that often.'

The mischievous side of the bright-eyed youngster's character certainly came through when the English Opera Group recorded an LP of the production; he munched nuts, not realizing that the microphones were picking up every tiny sound. Crawford still has the original score of *The Little Sweep*, complete with the composer's own notation.

After his success in the Britten production, a teacher at Oakfield School wrote a play for BBC schools radio and, during the next few years, the teenager appeared as actor or singer in hundreds of such broadcasts. The friendly rivalry with David Hemmings continued when they were both on radio in *The Little Beggars*, written by Ned Sherrin and Caryl Brahms[31]. 'Years later,' recalled Sherrin[32], 'he told me ruefully that he envied David Hemmings, then still a boy soprano, who played the child lead. Michael was livid that Hemmings, in the cloakrooms, seemed to be getting all the way with one of the girls while Crawford/Ingram was off in a corner with another girl – "simply practising how long we could kiss".'

In between these first ventures into showbusiness, the young hopeful was performing in a different way for audiences on the streets of South London, where he gained a reputation as the 'best egg-seller in Brixton'. He had been conducting this little enterprise since the age of twelve, wearing false moustaches and passing for sixteen. 'I was a favourite with the old ladies, as I used to save the brown eggs for them,' he said[33]. 'When I ran out, I'd paint the white ones brown!'

Chapter 2

TAKING THE BISCUIT

Leaving school at fifteen, intent on a career in showbusiness, Michael Ingram decided to change his name and was grateful to a passing biscuit lorry for solving this problem. Michael Crawford was born and, building on his stage and radio successes, he was soon starring in two productions for the Children's Film Foundation. This was an organization formed by film mogul J. Arthur Rank and financed since 1951 by the British film industry to make low-budget productions for screening at children's matinée performances, usually on Saturday mornings. Crawford, David Hemmings, Susan George, Judy Geeson, Olivia Hussey and Francesca Annis all started out on their film careers with the foundation.

Bushey Studios, in Hertfordshire, gave Crawford his first taste of acting for the big screen, although the thrills and spills in *Soapbox Derby* meant that plenty of fun was had at various locations in and around London. The story was about two rival South London gangs building soapbox cars to enter for a race. Crawford played Battersea Bats leader Peter Toms, complete with short trousers, who throws out one of his members, 'Foureyes' Fulton, blaming him when their plans for an exceptional car are stolen by Victoria Victors leader Lew Lender. Then the car itself is stolen and hidden in a quarry. 'Foureyes' is recruited by the Victoria Victors to improve its design, but the car is eventually discovered and wins the race for the Bats.

Nine Elms railway yard, next to the Thames in South London, was used as the location for the Battersea Bats' headquarters, a disused crane. It ensured lively lunchtimes for the railway workers, especially when Crawford had to jump into the river to rescue a member of the rival gang who had fallen in.

As in most Children's Film Foundation productions, there was an established 'grown-up' character actor. This time it was Harry Fowler, born in Lambeth but famous for playing cockneys. Here he was a barrow boy who became embroiled in a pitched battle with children in Wilcox Road market, South Lambeth. Stallholders and shopkeepers looked on with bemusement as he was pelted with bad fruit.

A week's filming at a sandpit near Leighton Buzzard, in Bedfordshire, where the Victors tried to destroy the Bats' car, was beset with difficulties when strong winds constantly filled actors' and technicians' eyes with sand, but the scenes were eventually completed to everyone's satisfaction. The exciting race sequences at the end of the film were shot at Crystal Palace.

One critic[1] described *Soapbox Derby* as 'a polished melodrama', adding, 'Most of the children have been directed to give very real, artless performances.'

The setting for Crawford's second Children's Film Foundation production, *Blow Your Own Trumpet*, was a Northern mining town and featured Peter Butterworth, well known for his appearances in children's television programmes. He played the kindly, old brass-band conductor who resigns after rowing with the father of a boy who wants to join the colliery band as a cornet player. He helps Crawford's character, Jim Fenn, who also wants to play the cornet in the band but does not have one, to buy the instrument and gives him lessons. Eventually Jim wins a competition and the conductor is reinstated.

Shot at Arley, near Coventry, and at Merton Park Studios, it was the foundation's first film to feature a brass band, in reality the award-winning Arley Welfare Band. 'One of the Children's Film Foundation's best, this film has a professional polish, and the children are expertly handled,' wrote one reviewer[2], who also remarked on the production's 'refreshing spontaneity'.

Still only sixteen, it looked as if acting would become the career for which Crawford had hoped. He was leaving behind ideas of training as a test pilot, which he had kept in mind as a second choice of career, although doubting that he would obtain the necessary academic qualifications. He continued to make radio broadcasts and took one of the lead roles in *Noye's Fludde*, based on the *Chester Miracle Play* and widely considered to be Benjamin Britten's masterpiece of children's music. This new work was premièred at Orford Church, near the composer's Suffolk home, as part of the Aldeburgh Festival[3], ten years after it began as a showcase for his works. The three performances all attracted more people than could be seated[4].

'Diapason' wrote in the *East Anglian Daily Times* of a full orchestra depicting the rising of the storm in this version of the biblical story of Noah, with bugles heard calling the creatures from the ark, followed by handbells ringing merrily. 'This,' he added, 'with a production characterised by a noble simplicity, could not fail to stir the emotions, deepened by the pure sincerity of starry-eyed child-actors. It was really quite marvellous to watch the ease and spontaneity of their movements and their naive reactions to fear, anguish, hope and liberation!'[5]

Colin Graham was making his debut as director of a new Britten production and, more than thirty years later, remembered that the composer had specially written one role for Crawford. 'Britten had written the part for him as the eldest son, Jaffet, which was a treble,' said Graham[6]. 'It came just at the time Michael's voice was breaking and Britten wanted him in that part, so he rewrote it as a young tenor. Michael showed that he was fulfilling all the promise we had seen in *Let's Make an Opera*.'

During the previous three years, Crawford had written hundreds of letters to producers and directors in his search for work, but it was his love of cycling – he sometimes rode from South London to Brighton and back in a day – that landed him his first work in repertory theatre. While he was out one day, a phone call was made to his Herne Hill home asking him to go straight to an audition at the Cambridge Theatre, London. He arrived back just twenty minutes before it was due to end.

'It would have taken forty-five minutes by bus, but I did it in a quarter of an hour by bike,' he said[7]. 'It was pouring with rain, but I couldn't bother about that. I ran into the theatre and did my piece straight away.' Producer James Roose-Evans and Bryan Bailey, director of the Belgrade Theatre, Coventry, were looking for a young actor to play the lead role in the French comedy *Head of the Family*. With five minutes to go, they had found him.

After starring in another radio play, *Children of the Arch-bishop*, Crawford arrived, with chaperon, in Coventry. The city had been devastated by German bombing during the Second World War and its newly built cathedral, which was to be a symbol of its phoenix-like rise from the ashes, was still awaiting the final touches before its opening. The Belgrade Theatre had already opened, in March 1958, the first civic theatre to be built in Britain since the war. It was housed in a block that included flats for the use of repertory company members, and it was here that Crawford managed to give his chaperon the slip for a couple of days, feeling that at sixteen he was old enough to look after himself.

'He was a very characterful boy, full of mischief,' recalled Patsy Byrne[8], a member of the company then and more recently known to millions of TV viewers as Mrs Stoneway in the comedy series *Watching*. 'He was bucking at having a chaperon at that age. I seem to remember he got away from her by locking himself in his flat with friends for the weekend and they had a jolly good party. I'm absolutely certain there was a crate of beer in there! He was very, very good in the play, but he was a little demon. Now, it would probably be regarded as good, but then it was seen as indiscipline.'

James Roose-Evans remembered another side to the young actor's personality. 'He was highly strung, easily depressed,' he said[9], 'but used to go round the theatre chanting to himself the words – which I believe he learned from Frank Finlay, who played his father in the play – "I must be resilient, *resilient!*" Frank, I think, had spoken to him about not taking everything that was said so personally but to learn how to ride the ups and downs, the vicissitudes, of theatre.' Roose-Evans recalled that, on stage, Crawford 'had even then a shining intensity and a quality of innocence, which made totally credible this adult fairy story of love and innocence, and made the play deeply poignant.'

The play, written by André Birabeau and set in the Paris of 1919, brought praise for the performances of Crawford and his co-star, nineteen-year-old Sarah Long, who had played the same role a year earlier when a different production was staged in Brighton and London. The young stars played sixteen-year-old lovers. He is the unloved schoolboy son of an unhappy marriage; she is an orphan. Together, they find contentment, then discover she is to

11

have his child. Their only fears are how to break the news to his well-to-do family and how to provide for the child.

'It owes much to acting of charm and conviction from Michael Crawford and Sarah Long as the boy and girl,' wrote the *Coventry Evening Telegraph* critic[10]. 'I could believe in these two, with feelings not of pity, but of admiration – as Birabeau surely intended. How they face their problems is a moving study of the confidence of youth and the perfection of simple love.' The *Birmingham Post*'s critic was not so enthusiastic about the production as a whole. 'After ten minutes,' wrote J.C.Trewin[11], 'the little piece became so predictable that it needed acting of quite uncommon quality to heighten it. We looked for this in vain, though I would not deny for a moment the complete sincerity of Michael Crawford and Sarah Long.'

The play also featured Richard Briers, as a doctor. After the production's two-week run in Coventry and a further week at the Oxford Playhouse[12], Frank Finlay – who played the father who ultimately realizes his failure – left the repertory company for America, where he appeared on Broadway in the short-lived John Osborne/Anthony Creighton play *Epitaph for George Dillon*[13]. During *Head of the Family*'s stage run, Sarah Long's agent, Adza Vincent, watched a performance and was so impressed with the promise shown by Crawford that she put him on her books.

After another appearance in *Noye's Fludde*, at Southwark Cathedral, Crawford returned to the Belgrade Theatre in a musical specially commissioned for the Christmas and New Year period. *Out of the Frying Pan*, a modern tale based on the Aladdin story, also saw the return of Frank Finlay and included Alan Howard, learning the ropes of acting as an assistant stage manager before later acclaim as a Royal Shakespeare Company member.

Set in the Frying Pan coffee bar, the production included not only a genie and magic lamp, but also teenagers who worshipped rock'n'roll, a military coup, flying saucers and flying sorcerers. A revolving stage with five sets helped to keep the pace fast and furious.

'So modern is this piece,' wrote *The Stage*[14], 'that part of the tale is played out on a giant "TV" screen which is but one of the wonders provided by a futuristic Merlin's time and talking-brain machine. This seasonal romp has everything: song, dance, drama, magic, laughs, romance, slapstick, farce, thrills. No genie need serve this talented, enthusiastic company. They perform wonders themselves.'

An unsporting *Stratford Herald* critic, leaving Shakespeare country for a night out in Coventry, could not bring himself to join in the fun. 'The play is a hotch-potch of fairytale and modern juvenile humour, which, even if it is only designed for children, has very little appeal,' he wrote[15]. 'The cast, with two exceptions, were not, to use the modern parlance of the dance halls, "with it". The exceptions were Michael Crawford as Nuri, the Prime Minister's son, who, from his first entrance, worked hard to give pace to this ponderous piece; Barbara Atkinson also amused as Millie the coffee-bar manageress, at times giving quite a credible imitation of Hylda Baker.'

Crawford's role as the young Etonian son of a Middle Eastern Prime Minister gave him a solo, sung to his schoolgirl love from his prison cell, that included the unforgettable line, 'Daphne, stop munching and spare me a thought.'

In March 1959, Crawford appeared in his third and final production at the Belgrade Theatre, playing Lucius in *Julius Caesar*, his and the company's first Shakespearean play. As the theatre approached its first anniversary, this proved to be one of its most successful plays.

Frederick Bartman, one of the stars of the legendary TV drama series *Emergency – Ward 10*, was brought in to play Cassius for the two-week run, with audiences boosted by local schoolchildren studying *Julius Caesar* for their English Literature exam. Unfortunately, they did not all take their studies very seriously and some of the bruising battle scenes, including a duel that went disastrously wrong on the first night, attracted misplaced laughter.

Chapter 3

WAITING FOR A BREAK

Returning to London, Crawford supplemented his income by working as a waiter at Lyons' Corner House, in Westminster, showing his athleticism by taking responsibility for a whole floor, a task normally given to four waiters. A television producer spotted him there and he was soon appearing in *Billy Bunter*[1]; there was also a one-off role in *Probation Officer*[2].

Crawford's first London stage play was *Change for the Angel*, at the small Arts Theatre Club, in Great Newport Street. When he went for the audition, playwright Bernard Kops and director David de Keyser had already cast Melvyn Hayes in the lead role and asked the star to read scenes with those trying for the other parts. Recalled Hayes:[3]

> One of the last guys to come along was this enthusiastic young man who was to play my elder brother, even though he was younger than me. He read a scene with me and I said: 'Just a moment,'
>
> I went down to the director and said: 'I think this boy could be very good.' So they booked him and we shared a dressing room.
>
> One of the things I remember about Michael was him waiting to make his entrance each night. He didn't walk on – he bounded on. It was as if someone had wound him up and released the key, like the spring of a watch.
>
> The money was dreadful. I was on the top salary, £11 a week, and he was on £9. They gave you half-a-crown each for

your lunch every day, four old pence for coffee and four old pence for tea in the afternoon. What you did was to save the lot up and cash it in for a big meal. The Arts Theatre was a club then and it was where all the unemployed actors used to hang out. You would hear them say, 'I was speaking to Larry last week.' They'd never even met Olivier, of course.

We did a four-week season. In those days, everything at the Arts Theatre used to be short runs. It was a good place to play: there was always a chance that you were going to transfer to a big West End theatre. If you acted there, you called it a West End theatre; if you were in Shaftesbury Avenue, you didn't. It's like off-Broadway in America, but it isn't like the difference between the West End and fringe – it's one step up from that.[3]

Change for the Angel was one of the increasing number of plays in the late Fifties and early Sixties to confront audiences with working-class culture. Author Bernard Kops had already made his name in theatre with *The Hamlet of Stepney Green*, another work of social concern, and later declared that theatre would never again be a 'precious inner sanctum for the precious few'[4]. Unfortunately, *Change for the Angel* was not one of his most acclaimed plays, suffering from too much purpose and not enough plot.

Set in a slum in Islington, North London, it showed the divisions in a working-class family where the boozing bully of a father resents the independence that the Welfare State has given to his three children. Melvyn Hayes played the younger son who wants to give up technical college and the chance of a job as an engineer so that he can fulfil his literary ambitions. Crawford was his elder brother, a flash local gang leader who prefers betting to honest work, and Jacqueline Forster was the sister who becomes pregnant by an American GI.

For all its sincerity, the play did not live up to the promise of its finely drawn characters and the *Manchester Guardian* called it 'a mildly glum artistic failure'[5]. Crawford was hardly mentioned in newspaper reviews and his appearance seemed to do him little harm.

His part in the 1960 British film *A French Mistress* was also largely unnoticed, but it was significant as his first step into the world of 'grown-up' films after his starring roles for the Children's Film Foundation. The stars this time were Cecil Parker, James Robertson Justice, Ian Bannen, Irene Handl and Kenneth Griffith. It was made by the famous Boulting Brothers, who had already begun ridiculing national institutions in comedies such as *Brothers In Law*, *Lucky Jim* and *I'm All Right, Jack*. Here the subject of farce was an English public school and the problems that follow when a beautiful female French teacher arrives and causes a sensation. Crawford played Kent, one of the boys who go on strike and threaten to burn down the gym when the headmaster decides to dismiss the teacher, who has fallen in love with his son – and whom he believes to be his illegitimate daughter. His fears eventually prove unfounded and she is reinstated, but not before the gym is ablaze.

The film was based on a saucy Twenties stage comedy by Robert Munro, better known as the late comedian Sonnie Hale[6], and it was not one of the Boulting Brothers' best, despite the presence of some great British character actors. Other 'schoolboys' included Jeremy Bulloch, who was to carve out a successful acting career, and Christopher Beeny, who had already made an impression as a child actor in *The Grove Family* TV serial and later appeared in programmes such as *Upstairs, Downstairs*, *The Rag Trade* and *In Loving Memory*.

More television work came with an episode of *Emergency – Ward 10*, then broadcast live. As a patient bandaged from head to foot, Crawford had to deliver only one line, but he forgot it, lifted the bed sheet to look down at a prompt card and uttered the immortal words, 'Have you seen this, nurse?'

A children's television series, *The Chequered Flag*, cast Crawford alongside Jeremy Bulloch, who had appeared with him in *Billy Bunter* and *A French Mistress*. The six episodes, broadcast on ITV in 1960, featured the two young actors as rivals on the racing circuit. 'Michael and I played budding racing drivers,' said Bulloch[7], 'so we started on the go-karts. I was the goodie and he wasn't exactly the baddie, but we were against each other all the time. In the story, I was the nicer one and would go on to be better than him in the end. We went to Silverstone to do a go-kart race before a meeting there, and we both said how lucky we were to get the roles of these boys. He was a cheerful chap and we got on terribly well. Michael has always been a perfectionist at his art. Even in those early days, he was very particular. I was beating him in the storyline, but he was, in reality, desperate to win all the races. It showed a little bit about his determination.'

Crawford's next film role was in the first Anglo-Swedish production, *Two Living, One Dead*. The idea was for Swedish studios to shoot films based on Scandinavian stories and aim them at an international market. This first venture, adapted from Norwegian writer Sigurd Christiansen's 1931 novel about the psychological effects on two post office clerks of an armed raid in which a colleague is killed, was beset with problems throughout filming and beyond. Following two previous film versions, by Swedish and Czech directors, there were high expectations of director Anthony Asquith and producer Teddy Baird.

Asquith, the son of former Liberal Prime Minister Herbert Henry Asquith, had started making films during the silent days and subsequently directed classics such as *Pygmalion*, *The Winslow Boy* and *The Browning Version*. Known as 'Puffin' since childhood because of his hooked nose, he had worked with Baird on four previous films and had just finished making *The Millionairess*, starring Sophia Loren, when he set off for Sweden in October 1960.

The stars were Virginia McKenna, her actor husband Bill Travers and Patrick McGoohan. McKenna had made her mark in films such as *A Town Like Alice* and *Carve Her Name With Pride*, and gave up acting in 1958 to look after her children. Now, with her husband playing the 'hero' survivor of the post office raid in *Two Living, One Dead*, she was persuaded to make a comeback, as the wife of the other, 'cowardly' survivor, played by McGoohan, already a star of films and the TV thriller series *Danger Man*. McKenna, Travers and McGoohan each earned £7,500 from the new film. Crawford, as a post office clerk further down the cast, was paid just £350 for five weeks' work[8].

Problems during the filming in Sweden included no official stills photographer to take publicity pictures during the early days of production, a fire at the hotel used by cast and crew, some film damaged during processing – and thick snow. When Crawford left for London, there was another five weeks' filming still to do, and that overran by a few days. During those final weeks, cameraman Gunnar Fischer[9] and Patrick McGoohan were struck down ill.

Director Asquith went down with lumbago on his New Year return to Sweden for editing conferences.

Alan Rothwell, who played another post office clerk in the film and soon afterwards became known on TV as David Barlow in *Coronation Street*, remembered Crawford as 'a good mate and good fun',[10] adding, 'We were both on a sort of level at the time. He was a good mimic and took off Virginia McKenna, Bill Travers and practically everyone in the cast. He did me as well, but never to my face. It was very hard to find things to do in Sweden. They were very short on bars, and the ones they had were dreadful, so scruffy. You sat down very glumly in a compartment, drank your beer and went out. Soon, we learned to play a card game called Racing Demon, which was what Anthony Asquith and Teddy Baird played. Every night, we had this session of playing this mad card game.'

This first, troubled venture into Anglo-Swedish films was completed, but it never received a British release[11]. In Sweden and Norway, countries more used to films exploring the human psyche, it was more warmly welcomed. 'In Anthony Asquith's delicate direction, the film has its power precisely in the care with which he presents the moral discussion of the novel,' wrote one critic[12]. 'The power of the film is in its fine characterizations.' Another reviewer wrote, 'This film has, without any doubt, preserved all the qualities of the novel and it is also very well performed.'[13]

Two Living, One Dead was seen by the British public only on television. Crawford was again in a small role that commanded little attention and he could count it as more experience on the ladder to success.

One person whose eye he did catch was Patrick McGoohan, who recommended him for the role of cabin boy John Drake in *Sir Francis Drake*, a twenty-six-part adventure series made by ITC, whose boss, Lew Grade, was expert at making programmes that would sell to America; one of them was *Danger Man*[14], starring McGoohan. Now, with *Sir Francis Drake*, Grade had the chance to sell a swashbuckling series across the Atlantic[15]. Terence Morgan and Jean Kent starred as Drake and Queen Elizabeth, and Crawford's character was the seaman's nephew. The programme was filmed at Associated British Elstree Studios, with a few outside scenes shot in Cornwall. A full-scale model of the *Golden Hind* was built to give the story as much authenticity as possible.

Peter Graham Scott, who made some episodes of *Danger Man* and the TV play *The Quare Fellow*[16], was working on the legendary series *The Troubleshooters* when he was called on to direct several episodes of *Sir Francis Drake*, including the opening one. 'The great thing about Michael,' he recalled[17], 'was that he never minded what you asked him to do. If I said I needed a member of the cast to be doused with a bucket of water, he would be the first to volunteer; he was game for anything. Working in the studio, you had to have buckets of water thrown over the actors to give the impression of being at sea!

'One episode was about Shakespeare performing on the deck to Queen Elizabeth. I decided this had to be done puristically and had a young boy dressed up as a girl in the play. Then I played a trick on Michael, who was a great chatter-up of girls at that time, and told him this person in costume was very keen on him, so he began to chat him up. Was his face red afterwards!'

Terence Morgan, who starred as the Elizabethan adventurer, also remembered the good spirit with which Crawford accepted such pranks. 'He always showed a good sense of fun and took a good deal of ribbing from the crew with the utmost charm and good humour,' said Morgan[18]. 'He was very popular on the set and worked very professionally. I recall very vividly how, after he had sung a short song in one of the episodes and commanded everybody's attention, he announced that he hoped one day to be able to play the lead in a big West End musical. He said this very seriously and with a hint of the single-mindedness and dedication he was eventually to show in realising this ambition. A lesser young man would almost certainly have been laughed at and called a big-head, but Michael had already shown us that, in spite of the clowning off set at work, he was a "pro", disciplined as well as talented, and quick as well as anxious to learn.'

Although made in black-and-white, *Sir Francis Drake* is still sold to television stations around the world. During 1990, Antenne 3, a new private TV company in Spain, was screening it[19]. Many familiar faces pop up during the twenty-six episodes, including Warren Mitchell, Glynn Edwards, Isobel Black, Nigel Davenport, Susan Hampshire, David McCallum, Patrick Allen, Barry Foster and Nanette Newman.

Steve McQueen's only British film, *The War Lover*[20], gave

Crawford his first real chance to shine on the big screen. The film, about the effect of war on young men at a United States Air Force base in Cambridgeshire during the Second World War, demanded that Crawford learn to speak with an American accent – in twenty-four hours. He went home and spent the night listening to a record by the West Coast comedian Woody Woodbury, learning the routines by heart until he had perfected the accent. At the audition, he ran through the gags in the same accent. The producer never laughed – perhaps he knew all the jokes – but Crawford landed the role of Junior Sailen.

During filming he became firm friends with Steve McQueen, who played a psychopathic, womanizing American bomber captain who tries to seduce his co-pilot's English girlfriend, only to be told a few home truths about his attitude to people and war. Shortly afterwards, during a bombing raid on Germany, his plane is damaged, he orders his crew to abandon the aircraft and he crashes suicidally into cliffs, his confidence having been smashed. While making this last scene, the stuntman standing in for Robert Wagner – playing McQueen's co-pilot – was killed while making the jump.

Before Crawford hit it off with McQueen, they had a confrontation on the set. 'I suppose I was cocky in those days, although inwardly nervous,' recalled Crawford[21]. 'Steve McQueen was evidently a bit worried that I wouldn't get the accent right and, just before my big scene, he came up to me and spoke to me about it. I used a few four-letter words. Afterwards, he said what a great kid I was.'

Based on the novel by John Hersey and also featuring British actress Shirley Anne Field, the film was a mish-mash of production, but McQueen's strong central performance and some exciting aerial bombing scenes held it together. 'Purely on an action level,' wrote the *Daily Cinema*[22], 'the aerial thrills – and especially the climactic raid which ends in tragedy – are strikingly staged.'

The action of the film was eclipsed by some of motor racing enthusiast McQueen's off-screen dramas, setting his Savoy Hotel room alight while trying to prepare himself a hamburger[23], driving at speed into the hotel's small forecourt and screeching into a U-turn – by hitting a large puddle on the way and drenching other guests[24] – and overturning his car while racing, against the film

20

studio's orders, resulting in a cut lip, which mean rescheduling some scenes[25].

Each day during filming, the supporting cast were picked up by limousines and taken to Shepperton Studios or Bovingdon RAF base in Hertfordshire. Some scenes were shot in Cambridge, but they did not involve Crawford. 'He behaved very much like the character he was playing, and everybody treated him like the character, the young kid,' recalled Chuck Julian[26], an actor in the film who has since become a theatrical agent. 'He was looked upon as the younger brother in a family is. Everybody in the crew of that plane became a family, and he was the junior. He thought he was the odd man out as far as nationality was concerned because everybody else, including me, was North American. He was the one Englishman playing an American.

'A lot of us used to play poker on the set or in the aircraft hangars on location. Michael never joined in; I don't think it was his scene. He thought we were all depraved gamblers. Even though he wasn't a poker player, he tried to be one of the guys and belong to the group.

'Michael was a bit of a practical joker. One time, somebody went looking for him all over the place. He couldn't be seen in his dressing-room; he couldn't be found anywhere on the set; he wasn't in the canteen. Then, we thought we heard a noise in the wardrobe in his dressing-room. I opened one of the doors and Al Waxman opened the other, and there was Michael sitting on the floor in the wardrobe. I thought: "What a daft bugger!" He thought it was hilarious.'

Despite this extroversion, Chuck Julian remembered Crawford as being shy. 'Again, that was like the character he played,' said Julian[27]. 'I think this was probably borne out of the insecurity of inexperience. There was one scene in the film where the rest of the crew goaded his character into asking out a bar girl on a date, but he was so shy and embarrassed. Later, when he was in the gun under the plane, he got shot up.'

Crawford, who turned twenty while *The War Lover* was being made, was now being noticed. During the next year he would have major roles in theatre, film and television.

Chapter 4

BLOWING HIS HORN

With his accomplished American accent, Crawford went for a part in the London stage version of the Broadway hit comedy *Come Blow Your Horn*, which became *Sergeant Bilko*[1] TV writer Neil Simon's first West End play. He landed the role of Buddy Baker, the shy younger son of a New York Jewish family who turns into a playboy. The accent was good enough to fool Canadian-born Bernard Braden, who had appeared in *The War Lover* but had not met Crawford during the filming, into thinking he really was American. 'I was at the first-night party of *Come Blow Your Horn*,' said Braden[2], 'and remember being completely fooled by his American accent in the play, so I was very surprised to hear him talking in an English accent afterwards.'

Crawford had been the last actor to audition for the role of Buddy. Detesting auditions and unsure of what to do, he nervously sang 'God Save the Queen'. Bob Monkhouse, best known as a comedy writer and actor for television and radio, and playing his first straight acting role in the West End, as Buddy's elder brother, Alan, spotted Crawford's comedy potential and invited him to his home, where they spent an evening reading the play.

Come Blow Your Horn ran at the Prince of Wales Theatre for eighteen months. David Kossoff, who played the Baker brothers' father, still remembers the impression that Crawford left on him. 'When we started to rehearse, I had never heard of this slim, fair, rather shy person,' he recalled[3]. 'As the shier and more uncertain of the two brothers, his problem wasn't to be wimpish but to be funny, and he knew immediately that the comedy had to come

22

up out of the character, not just out of what he said. That was instinct.

'I watched him working out his comedy and immediately recognized a considerable talent. I have never forgotten that I came home to my wife and said: "There's a young man working with us and I'm sure he is going to be a big star." He was always delightful to work with and very disciplined.'

Crawford's performance, for which he was paid £30 a week, also won praise from theatre critics. 'Michael Crawford contributes a fine comic performance as the virgin boy blossoming into a playboy,' wrote Robert Muller in the *Daily Mail*[4]. Although the *Daily Telegraph*'s reviewer thought the twenty-year-old too young for the role of Buddy, he conceded that 'he plays it with an infectious sense of fun'[5]. The actor's crowning glory came when he was presented with *Variety*'s London Theatre Critics' Award for Most Promising Newcomer of 1963.

His first starring role in a film as an adult, in *Two Left Feet*, brought frustration. 'It was to be,' he recalled[6], 'the first of the kitchen-sink comedies, but, unfortunately, it was not released for three years, making it the last of the kitchen-sink comedies.' The film did not reach cinemas until 1965 because of a hold-up in the release of productions distributed by British Lion.

Based on David Stuart Leslie's novel *In My Solitude*, the story cast Crawford in the clumsy 'two left feet' role for which he soon became familiar. He played Alan Crabbe, a nineteen-year-old who falls for the older Eileen – played by Nyree Dawn Porter – and is later beaten up by her fiancé. Eileen breaks off her engagement, but Alan then resumes his relationship with the younger Beth, played by Julia Foster. Also in the cast was Crawford's old sparring partner from Benjamin Britten days, David Hemmings.

A well-observed story, with admirable performances, *Two Left Feet* gave Crawford some comical scenes that were a prelude to his later role as Frank Spencer on television. When his character leaps at Eileen after taking her home from a jazz club, he starts a chain reaction involving a dog, all the cats in the district, crying babies, shouting neighbours and the sound of breaking glass. In the hullabaloo, he creeps away from the row of houses, silhouetted against the night sky. Later, bumping something against the bannister in the house of Beth's mother, he says, 'Sorry, madam, you know how it is. We take no pride in our work these days.'

As a young romeo, Crawford had to look the part. 'I wore my first suit, combed my hair flat and tried to look as near Cary Grant as possible,' he recalled[7], 'but I came out looking more like Lassie.' So self-conscious was he that he was banned from seeing the 'rushes', the daily lengths of film shot.

When *Two Left Feet* was eventually released, critics pointed out that it had become dated, but there was general praise for the performances of Crawford and his two female co-stars, all of whom had been unknown when they made the film but had become names by the time it was shown in cinemas. 'Michael Crawford takes his induction into the ways of the world with his usual incredulous gape,' wrote Eric Shorter in the *Daily Telegraph*[8], adding cautiously, 'It is a pity to see a young and promising actor always playing the same role, though he is undoubtedly quite good at it.'

With most of 1962 and 1963 taken up with stage, television and film work, Crawford could reflect that his career was moving in the right direction. His professional contentment was muted by personal sadness with the death of his mother, aged just forty-four[9], during the run of *Come Blow Your Horn*, his first real success. 'What pleased me most about that,' he said[10], 'was that my mother knew about it before she died, so she could see I was getting somewhere.'

One of the most exciting events in provincial theatre since the war was the opening of the new Nottingham Playhouse in December 1963. Crawford returned to repertory work to be there for the first three months, appearing alongside stars such as Leo McKern, who had turned down two films and offers from the National Theatre and the Royal Shakespeare Company to go to Nottingham, and classical actor John Neville, who had just starred in *Alfie* on the London stage and was giving up £200-a-week West End rates for the £20 to £50 Playhouse level. That was a measure of the support this new venture enjoyed. Ian McKellen was also there, in his early theatre days, before winning national acclaim.

The building of the new theatre, replacing the old Playhouse, had been a long-running political battle. Started by the local

Labour council, the plans were cancelled on financial grounds when the Tories took over, but building was allowed to continue after negotiations to sell the site fell through.

It was intended to be the National Theatre of the provinces, attracting top actors and directors. Crawford did not come into that category, but the memory of performing there in Shakespeare's *Coriolanus* and Oscar Wilde's *The Importance of Being Earnest* was a particularly happy one. He was exhilarated by working with the legendary director Sir Tyrone Guthrie in the Shakespearean tragedy, in which he had the humble roles of Second Servingman and Second Citizen. 'I only had a tiny part in *Coriolanus*,' he said a few years later[11], 'but it was the most exciting experience I've ever had in the theatre.'

Coriolanus was the new Playhouse's first production. Afterwards, Crawford and the rest of the cast were presented to Lord Snowdon, who performed the theatre's official opening ceremony, standing in for his then wife, Princess Margaret. At a civic reception, blows were exchanged between one of the town clerk's staff and a stage worker, after members of the company arrived to find no food left[12]. Verbal battles followed in the columns of local newspapers, reminiscent of the rows that took place during the five-year struggle to build the theatre.

On stage, the results were pleasing. 'By the end of the last act I was swearing that this was the most marvellous *Coriolanus* in every conceivable way that I should ever hope to see,'wrote T. C. Worsley in the *Financial Times*[13].

Crawford was featured more prominently in *The Importance of Being Earnest*, as Algernon Moncrieff. Unfortunately this play was overshadowed by the opening production and Crawford was the only leading actor not to merit a mention from Eric Shorter in the *Daily Telegraph*, who believed that the key to performing this wittiest of farces was in the technique. 'The senior members of the Nottingham company clearly and delightfully have it,' he wrote[14]. 'But time and again, chances for wit are lost through faulty emphasis, sheer inaudibility or reluctance to let us anticipate a line.'

Ronald Magill, who later became known to millions of television viewers as Amos Brearly in *Emmerdale*[15], was then an actor at the Nottingham Playhouse, as well as its associate director, and spoke the first words in the new theatre. 'I think Michael was probably miscast in *The Importance of Being Earnest*,' he recalled[16], 'but, in *Coriolanus*, he made much of a small part. As a servant, he had to be rushing around, and he was a bit Chaplinesque in what he did – everything was so neat and detailed.

'He gave it his all, such energy and dedication. Tyrone Guthrie was a great one for comic business, and it was amazing to see how Michael picked it all up. Guthrie said to me: "This boy's going to be a star." Off stage, I just remember him as being extraordinarily friendly and like a puppy, frolicking about and full of good spirits.'

Ken McReddie, an actor and assistant stage manager at the Playhouse, who has since become a theatrical agent, remembered Crawford being 'very energetic and noticeably good', but there were other memories, too. 'He was a callow youth then, but he had a very strong personal presence,' he recalled[17]. 'Also, he did a lot of giggling on stage. The audience might not have noticed, but the other actors were aware of it.' Although generally popular with members of the company, Crawford left Leo McKern with 'the remaining impression of a young man with an inflated self-opinion regarding his importance', although McKern added[18], 'However, he was obviously quite correct in this regard.'

While performing in Nottingham, Crawford paid minimal rent by living on the top floor of a brothel. 'The madam would have had me if I hadn't escaped by telling her the lodger in the room next door to mine fancied her like crazy,' he said[19].

It was a cold winter, and he soon found out that the theatre was centrally heated and the heating in his dressing-room was on throughout the day and night, so he moved in. Some other members of the company decided this was a good idea, too. When Christmas came round, many of them stayed there for the festivities. It was Crawford's first after the death of his mother, and other actors could not afford to travel back to their families.

Christmas lunch was to be prepared in the theatre kitchens and Crawford volunteered to take charge. Pleading poverty, he sought charity from local shopkeepers, and a butcher gave him an enormous turkey, which might actually have been a small emu. It was Christmas Eve and, during the interval in *Coriolanus* that night, he put the bird in the oven, expecting it to take fourteen hours to cook.

'In the end,' he recalled[20], 'it took eighteen hours to cook and an hour-and-a-half to carve. There were no chairs or tables in the kitchens, so we ate it standing up around the cookers and stoves. We had also managed to scrounge plenty of drink and, as we had the whole theatre to ourselves, we played endless games of paper chase and treasure hunt in and out of the stalls and the boxes and the circle. We were just like children let loose.'

On Boxing Day, three actors were missing from the matinée performance of *The Importance of Being Earnest*. They had passed out as a result of the good time had by all and did not come to until the evening.

Moving swiftly on, after three months in Nottingham, Crawford appropriately spent March 1964 touring the country as Glaydon in *March Hares*, a new, surrealistic comedy by Ronald Harwood that starred Ian Carmichael. Following his success in *Come Blow Your Horn*, theatre work was becoming more regular, and Crawford joined the New Shakespeare Company for an eight-week tour of *Twelfth Night*, which took him across England and to three venues in Portugal. He played Feste, and the cast included Annette Crosbie as Viola and Frederick Bartman as Malvolio.

The tour finished with four days at the Middle Temple, one of the Inns of Court, resplendent with oak, stained glass and armorial plaques. The performance formed part of the Festival of the City of London. The Middle Temple was where Elizabeth I was reputed to have attended the first documented performance of *Twelfth Night*, in 1602, although there is now doubt about this. However, during July 1964, Queen Elizabeth the Queen Mother was there for the opening night.

Crawford had not been the first choice to play Feste, until Colin Graham – who directed him in Benjamin Britten productions – was brought in. 'I wanted him in the first place,' said Graham[21], 'but the management had already cast Cy Grant. I had previously directed Cy in a musical, but there is a big difference between a musical and Shakespeare's text. Halfway through rehearsals, we realized he couldn't cut it. Cy left the cast and Michael came in for the last two weeks of rehearsals. I had no doubts that he could deal with Shakespeare's text. I had seen *Come Blow Your Horn* and kept my eye on what he was up to, and I knew he was the right person for that part. He was the same Michael, but grown up, and just as engaging and delightful to work with as when he was a kid.'

Graham's production, performed on a mock-up apron stage, included wistful music written by Johnny Dankworth and slapstick comedy, which gave Crawford the chance to get noticed for what he did best. 'Although Mr Crawford does not impress any firmness of personality on Feste,' wrote *The Times*'s critic[22], 'the comic scenes, with Mr Stephen Moore's Sir Andrew joining wholeheartedly in the romp, are disciplined and not uninventive.'

Stephen Moore also provided the guitar accompaniment to the songs. He and Crawford got together and organized their own stage act, which included a few of their own songs. 'We both wrote the music and used Shakespeare's words,' recalled Moore[23]. 'We used Johnny Dankworth's songs as well and talked about the play and about acting. In Oxford, we did the act at the Playhouse sometime during the evening of the *Twelfth Night* performance, and in Coimbra, in Portugal, we found a university. We simply did it to amuse people. I was accompanying him in the show anyway and I think we just had the nerve.'

Chapter 5

THE KNACK/BYRON

During 1964 Crawford made *The Knack ...and how to get it*, his first of three films with director Richard Lester, who had been a writer of *The Goon Show* on radio and had taken that brand of surrealism to film-making, using a new-wave style that reflected the mood of the Swinging Sixties and the idea that the world was being turned upside down.

Lester had just made the Beatles film *A Hard Day's Night* and was to follow *The Knack* with another Fab Four production, *Help!* When Crawford auditioned for *The Knack*, producer Oscar Lewenstein asked him whether he had any previous experience. 'You don't have to be an actor to make films,' Crawford replied[1]. 'It just so happens that I am.' His point was that films were a director's medium and he quoted *A Hard Day's Night* as a good example of a director working with non-actors. 'I didn't know the man sitting next to the producer was Dick Lester, who had just directed that film,' recalled Crawford[2]. 'Anyway, I got the part and it certainly couldn't have been my charm or personality that did it.'

The film, written by Charles Wood, was based on Ann Jellicoe's stage play, and Crawford was cast as Colin, a shy teacher who envies the success with women enjoyed by his lodger Tolen, played by Ray Brooks. As he gradually learns 'the knack' himself, he wins over Nancy, Rita Tushingham's character, from Tolen. Donal Donnelly was also featured, as Tom, another lodger. Richard Lester recalled:

I deliberately didn't see the play because there's always a

danger in getting too obsessed with what was on the stage and feeling you mustn't tamper with it when you translate it to film. My only memory of those auditions was that everyone seemed to have a better idea of why they were perfect for each particular part than I did! I hadn't seen Michael before, which is normal for me. I have a tendency to cast people by talking to them, rather than seeing their work, on the assumption that if you have a good casting director they don't send you rubbish. You look for qualities that match the actor to the character.

Charles Wood and I worked quite a long time to explore the framework of *The Knack* and take away a lot of the theatrical implications. In truth, that affected the casting of Tolen rather than Michael's character, Colin. Being a physical actor was one of Michael's obvious qualities and there was no doubt that I was looking to do a very physical piece. It needed a kind of gauche innocence, which Michael was able to produce and project quite well. In the end, Colin had to develop a strength of character, of steel, as opposed to the others, who didn't develop. Michael had an assuredness, despite the fact that he was a very young man.[3]

Shot in black-and-white, the picture was a fast-moving set of zany jokes – including visual gags such as its stars wheeling an iron bed frame through the streets of London – intercut with asides from members of the public, the older generation commenting on the collapse of public morals.

It was the vehicle for which Crawford had been looking. 'Although it was an ensemble piece,' said Richard Lester[4], 'I felt that Michael and Rita Tushingham were the co-leads because we structured the film more around the two of them than did the play, which was a fairly even four-hander.'

Lester was quick to point out that his style of film-making, which at times appeared like a documentary in its realism, did not allow for improvization. 'There's always the implication that if a film has a fairly exuberant quality that there's some improviz-ation,' he said[5]. 'There was no improvization at all. There was no way you could add a word of dialogue, because it was all a series of interlacing farces. There's one scene of four minutes where every third or fourth sentence is "What about the cases?", referring to what Rita's character was going to do with her baggage, and it changes so that each person is saying it with a different meaning. This was absolutely stylized.'

Filming took place in a Victorian house in Shepherd's Bush; the back of it was used as the production office and the front of it for filming. Dozens of locations in and around London were also used. Some of the street scenes had to be 'snatched' because the crew had no police co-operation and were constantly moved along[6]. To get all the shots needed for these quick 'takes', Lester had two cameras filming the action and a third, hidden, focusing on the faces of frowning passers-by. To this third set of pictures he added appropriate disapproving comments and cut them into the action. The results were stunningly successful and caught the flavour of Sixties London and the generation gap.

The Knack also provided Crawford with the opportunity to do the sort of daredevil stunts for which he would later become famous. Here he had to water-ski. 'Michael had never water-skied before,' recalled director of photography David Watkin[7]. 'He spent the morning learning while we shot something else. After lunch, we filmed Michael on water skis doing some hair-raising things.'

More than twenty-five years later, Richard Lester remembered vividly the extent of Crawford's achievement that day. 'Charles Wood and I were not aware of the problems when we wrote the scene,' he recalled[8]. 'Michael was on a dock, fully dressed in tweed jacket, tie, trousers and hush-puppies, and had to put on a pair of water skis, be pulled off the dock into the water, by a rope attached to a motorboat that roared past, and ski away. Normally when you start water-skiing, you are lying in the water with your skis up in the air and the boat goes slowly away and you slowly come up, but this was like being catapulted into the water.

'We went to one of those old gravel pits where they do water-skiing. I think it was the head of the British water-skiing team who ran the camp and got us the boats and the equipment. When we described what we wanted to do, he said, "That's totally impossible. I've got five or six people here who have been water-skiing all their lives, and there's no way any of them can do it." Michael said: "I can do it." He said: "You're wasting your time. You'll have to trick it somehow." We said: "We will have a go."

31

'The first time, Michael went in and was dragged underwater for a bit. The second 'take' was perfect. They said nobody could do it. It was astonishing that he knew he could do it. There was no real risk or danger – he would just have been buffeted, not seriously hurt. But that was the first case of that absolute determination which he was to use to great effect in the later films I did with him.'

Only twelve seconds of Crawford's newly found skill was seen in this racy film and, incidentally, one of the two female water-skiers glimpsed in the same scene was Charlotte Rampling in her first film role.

'Dick Lester really encouraged me to develop myself,' said Crawford[9]. 'Mind you, I wouldn't follow a director to the devil. I know my limitations and most of my security comes from hard-learned technical expertise. It's only after I've mastered the basic moves that I can begin to concentrate on the emotions.'

Lester had discovered an actor whom he admired and believed would become a major star. 'Because I'm always terribly involved in visual comedy,' he said[10], comparing the film's two leading characters, 'it was much easier to deal with Michael Crawford's character, Colin. When Colin is upset, all you have to do is have him with a teacup in his hand and his trousers not quite fitting. Colin must win because he is the physical buffoon; he falls into traps and puts his head through walls, falls downstairs and all those things.'

In 1965 *The Knack* was shown at film festivals around the world and won the top prize at Cannes, the Palme D'Or. On its release in Britain, the *Daily Worker* described it as 'the first genuine "mod" film of the British cinema'[11] and the *Sunday Express* declared that 'its real jewels are the shining performances of Michael Crawford, as the gauche youth, and Miss Tushingham, as the girl who gives him the knowledge'[12]. The film also won rave reviews in America and made Crawford known on both sides of the Atlantic.

International acclaim was preceded by fame on British television as the motor-scooter rider Byron, who delivered a weekly monologue reflecting the views of Britain's youth in the BBC satirical series *Not So Much a Programme, More a Way of Life*. Crawford did only a dozen spots of four minutes each during late 1964 and early 1965, but the impact was such that viewers remembered the character for years afterwards.

The idea evolved when producer Ned Sherrin was looking for a sequel to *That Was the Week That Was*, the irreverent series that dared to poke fun at the Establishment and made stars of David Frost, Roy Kinnear, William Rushton, Eleanor Bron and Millicent Martin. *Not So Much a Programme* was to be broadcast on Friday, Saturday and Sunday nights. Frost and Bron returned as regular members of the team and were joined by Patrick Campbell, Roy Hudd, John Wells, Doug Fisher and, for a short time, Leonard Rossiter.

Scriptwriters Peter Lewis and Peter Dobereiner decided there should be a character who could put into words what young people were thinking. He would be based on Holden Caulfield, the fictional character of J.D.Salinger's funny-sad novel *The Catcher In the Rye*, which told the story of a teenager driven to despair by the phoniness and hypocrisy of the adult world, and created a huge impact on its publication in the Fifties.

Ned Sherrin thought the ideal actor for the role would be Crawford, whom he had seen in *Come Blow Your Horn* and *Twelfth Night*. He later realized that, as a child, Michael Ingram had been in *The Little Beggars*, a radio play that was his and Caryl Brahms's first script to be performed, starring Alec McCowen[13], with David Hemmings as the child lead.

When Crawford went to Sherrin's London home to discuss the role of Byron, the producer was surprised by his attitude. 'It is usual for young, little-known actors to grasp at chances of solo exposure on a probably fashionable, potentially long-running television series,' recalled Sherrin[14]. 'Michael showed no instinct to conform. He grilled me severely about the attitude and background of the character, the place he would occupy in the programme, his point of view, and innumerable other aspects of Byron which I had not yet thought about.'

Crawford would not move until he was satisfied on all points. He eventually left after Sherrin agreed to send him a script. 'I think he came to audition *me*,' reflected Sherrin, with a smile[15]. 'He is a perfectionist and is terribly demanding. He still does it; he doesn't accept *jobs* – he accepts jobs on his own terms.'

Byron was an immediate success in the Sunday-night programme, giving his views on sex, religion, the National Health Service, the BBC and other topical subjects. Everything was 'turgid' and he was 'smashed to fragments' by some events, but writer Peter Dobereiner sensed that Crawford sometimes did not relate to his and Peter Lewis's scripts. 'He had difficulty handling the material,' recalled Dobereiner[16]. 'He didn't always understand the issues of the day that he was talking about. He was very good when it was subjects he understood, like girlfriends or summer holidays, but when we brought in a political issue he wasn't quite so sure of it, but he grew into it very well. He was very nervous to start with, which was funny because he was enormously self-assured professionally. He was just a young kid thrown into this — very professional, but slightly naive.'

Crawford became protective towards the character of Byron. 'I adopted what I conceived to be a classless accent,' he said[17], 'as that is what I thought Byron ought to be and that is what I am. It was a mixture of Wiltshire, Cheshire, London and Kent.' Sherrin recalled the actor occasionally phoning in with ideas for the monologues, but Crawford's desire to deliver a eulogy to Sir Winston Churchill after the wartime Prime Minister's funeral met with a cold response from his producer.

'All through the day of the funeral,' said Sherrin[18], 'the solemnity, the pomp and the processing poured out of the television and Michael, who was sitting at home watching it all, was inspired to address the nation through the character of Byron and to explain the impact on his generation of discovering the greatness of the dead ex-Prime Minister. It was difficult enough to find an appropriate way of treating Churchill's funeral without having to cope with an actor who felt moved to speak about it on behalf of the youth of Britain. I was a bit short with him, and this incident finds no place in Michael's lexicon of great lessons learned early.'

Crawford had already clashed with Sherrin when told one week that Lewis and Dobereiner's script was, unusually for them, not up to standard and, although he would be paid, he would not appear unless they provided a better one. 'They failed to do so,' said Sherrin[19], 'and Michael fretted and fumed and explained that his immense following of fans would be mortified and he would be shamed. Finally, he had to be sent home in a tantrum.' Later, Crawford generously conceded to Sherrin that the decision was right and it was a lesson in not using substandard material.

The popularity of Byron was also a warning to Crawford, who

saw the danger of becoming typecast. 'It was quite a useful job at the time,' he said[20], 'but restrictive. I wouldn't have wanted it to go on too long. Money and security can be a temptation, but you've got to be firm and know when to turn off from what could be a blind alley.'

By appearing in only the Sunday episode of *Not So Much a Programme*, Crawford had been able to continue with other work, which included a run of *The Striplings* on stage at the New Arts Theatre Club, in London. In this play by new writer Nina Warner Hooke, he acted the public school-educated Biff, who, with his sister, inherits a riding school when their mother dies and ponders how they can run it in their poverty. The fifteen-year-old sister, Jojo, played by Karin Fernald, is later revealed to be getting supplies for the stable by servicing the farmers of the district.

'Michael Crawford has a most effective and moving last scene as the drunken brother unable to forgive the corruption of his sister,' wrote Milton Shulman in the London *Evening Standard*[21]. Reviews were mixed, but there was general praise for Crawford. 'Of a four-handed cast,' wrote Bernard Levin in the *Daily Mail*[22], 'Mr Michael Crawford, as the brother who cannot bear his sister to be touched by the world, makes a great deal out of what I suspect is not very much, conveying well his uncomprehending self-disgust.'

In April 1965 Crawford opened with Harry H. Corbett in a new comedy, *Travelling Light*, at the Prince of Wales Theatre, where he had enjoyed such success in *Come Blow Your Horn*. Corbett, who had a string of classical roles behind him[23] but was best known as the star of *Steptoe and Son* on TV[24], played a married travelling salesman, Brian, who is having an affair and aches for his lover after a fortnight's absence, only to find himself sharing a bed-sitting room with a religious zealot, Arnold, played by Crawford. Julia Foster, who starred with Crawford in *Two Left Feet*, which was finally released during the play's run, was cast as Brian's prim girlfriend, Tricia, horrified by the idea of making love in the same room as a stranger. The farce begins when Arnold falls for her.

'The play is trite,' wrote the *Sunday Express*[25], 'but it is given a stature it doesn't deserve by Mr Crawford's superb, utterly beguiling, beautifully timed, thoroughly convincing performance. He is a joy to watch.' Milton Shulman, in the London *Evening Standard*, described Crawford and Corbett's acting as 'two of the neatest comic performances I have seen in the West End for some time'[26]. He added, 'Michael Crawford, gangling, gauche and trying to escape from life through Oriental mysticism, achieves some really hilarious effects with his alternating bouts of unworldly chatter and inexplicable rage.'

Professionally, Crawford's career was going from strength to strength, and his association with film director Richard Lester continued with *A Funny Thing Happened On the Way To the Forum*. Unfortunately Lester did not have complete artistic control over the picture. Producer Melvin Frank, who had scripted several Bob Hope films and co-wrote this with Michael Pertwee, originally intended to direct the screen version of the hit musical comedy himself. He handed over to Lester but was unwilling to let the director make many of the changes he felt were necessary.

Frank had signed up Zero Mostel and Jack Gilford – from the original stage show[27] – and Phil Silvers. Lester added to them Crawford, Buster Keaton, Sir Michael Hordern and Roy Kinnear, and began the hazardous task of amending the script and Stephen Sondheim's musical numbers. Frank was brought up in the Hollywood studio tradition and expected producers to exert a large amount of control, but Lester's lack of freedom did not stop him changing parts of the script – including all of Crawford's scenes – and reducing the number of songs.

The difference was in approach. Frank wanted a bawdy stage comedy transferred to film; Lester wanted to go more deeply into the subject, the cruelties and shabbiness of first-century Rome. He also saw the need to rewrite roles around the talents of the actors, as he did for Crawford, but there were limits to what he could do to make the most of the story for the cinema. The film was seen by many critics as Lester's least satisfactory during that period, but it was probably far better than he believed at the time, while embroiled in battles with Frank.

Certainly, it had all the makings of a cinematic success: a superb international cast in the roles of cheating, lying slaves, beautiful handmaidens and courtesans, broad-shouldered, not-too-bright soldiers, henpecked husbands, domineering wives, long-lost children and vestal virgins, involved in love and death scenes, processions, chases and a slave market. This was not the Rome of the emperors, but a little one-round-the-corner.

'I was quite a young man,' said Lester[28], 'and Melvin Frank was quite experienced and assumed that I would act as a kind of surrogate director. I didn't see the piece the way he did; there were serious problems. I had surreptitiously to do major rewrites three or four weeks before shooting, which was a bit ridiculous, but I felt I had to. To cast Michael as a juvenile lead and leave him to do nothing but singing, as the part was on stage, would have been crazy. I went to my house in Madrid with Nicolas Roeg, the lighting cameraman, and we worked on rewriting the script. Ultimately, we managed to produce a film which is half the original and half ours – and, unfortunately, it shows.'

Filming began on a windy Spanish hillside at Las Matas, fifteen miles outside Madrid, in August 1965. Over the next four months, the weather veered from intense heat to snowstorms. Lester turned down the offer of using a set already constructed and used for *The Fall of the Roman Empire*, saying that he could not afford the rental for the scaffolding. 'I looked across and found another hill, more of a slum,' he said[29]. 'We did a set for a musical on a series of mounds and hills. It drove the producer mad! He was a Hollywood man, used to having huge cranes going up and down for musicals.' The new set recreated a section of ancient Rome that comprised five streets of fountains, shops, a bakery, a slave market and a chariot repair shop. Interior filming was done at Bronston Studios, in Madrid.

Lester, with cameraman Nicolas Roeg, managed to stamp his mark on the film by employing quick cutting from one scene to another and sight gags that included Crawford tying a love note to a pigeon and watching the bird promptly plummet to the ground. Less successful was Buster Keaton, in his last screen role shortly before his death. Throughout the film there are brief glimpses of him, as Erronius, running around Rome's Seven Hills searching for his kidnapped children.

'Some people thought the film was too quick and too frenetic,' said Lester[30]. 'That was partly because you couldn't hold on given scenes in the way you would normally do. We had to "double" a lot of Keaton's work because he was quite ill and had difficulty in breathing, and therefore had difficulty in running. So we used a "double". Normally, you could have filmed a sequence where he was running, then stopped to speak, in one go, but it involved six or seven "cuts". To allow Buster only to speak and not to move seemed to be the height of folly.'

The film was a disappointment, although it did win the Golden Gate Award at the 1966 San Francisco Festival, as well as winning Ken Thorne an Oscar for Best Music Adaptation. Recognizing the contradictions in the film, *Variety* wrote, 'Though the story is soon submerged under the unburdensome weight of production numbers, tricky visuals, sight gags and numerous bits, their expert mechanics and overall cleverness excuse the interruptions. Lester's direction, despite his operational mode, which is something akin to silent film lensing (each day's lensing must produce a completed "bit"), is finally approaching the ability to collect sight gags into a cohesive and structured whole. The strain, however, sometimes shows through, periodically degenerating into pastiche, obscuring scripts and performances.'[31]

Chapter 6

FAMILIES

After his mother's death, Crawford parted company with his stepfather for ever and moved in with his maternal grandmother, Edith Pike. 'I felt a bit lost in the world and had no brothers or sisters,' he recalled[1], 'so my gran and I sort of adopted each other. She was getting on in years, and I was very fond of her.'

When he found a small flat in London, he invited her to stay with him; it had only one bedroom but two beds. Later, while riding on the crest of a wave as the gormless Frank Spencer on television, Crawford had an annexe built on to his Bedfordshire cottage and his grandmother lived there until she died, at the age of ninety-eight.

It was a good age for someone who had seen untimely deaths on all sides of her family. Born Edith Keefe in Londonderry, Northern Ireland, after her first husband died she married a lance corporal in the Military Foot Police, in Southampton during the last year of the First World War[2]. Seven months later, daughter Doris was born[3] and was herself to experience widowhood at a young age, followed by a second marriage.

Crawford was reluctant to marry, despite a long-term relationship with hairdresser Patricia Mansell. After six years together, they split up and, on 8 December 1965, she gave birth to their daughter, Angelique Simone Avison[4]. 'Women are a great idea,' Crawford had said the previous year[5], 'but I don't go for this marriage bit. Work's very important to me and if the love affair isn't working I can't be happy at work.'

During 1965, Crawford met former dancer Gabrielle Lewis,

who had trained as an actress at drama school and appeared in a few stage plays. She was working by night as a disc-jockey at the Pickwick Club, in London, which was owned by actors Anthony Newley and Harry Secombe. 'Michael was in a play in London and he came in and kept asking me to play Donovan's *Catch the Wind*,' recalled Gabrielle[6].

Crawford, who was appearing on stage in *Travelling Light*, was being urged by fellow-star Harry H. Corbett to ask Gabrielle to dance, instead of just staring at her, but he was too tongue-tied. Eventually, after three weeks, he stepped in to rescue her from another, unwanted admirer and love blossomed.

He set off for Spain in August 1965 to film *A Funny Thing Happened On the Way To the Forum* with director Richard Lester. During the four-month schedule, Crawford proposed over the phone to Gabrielle, who was pregnant. 'I remember a lot of three and four o'clock in the morning phone calls,' recalled Lester[7]. 'Michael was anxious to get it sorted out and asked me to arrange the wedding.'

The ceremony, which took place on 20 December, after filming had finished, was at the British Embassy in Paris – 'That seemed to be the most discreet way,' said Lester[8] – and was a slightly comic affair. It had to be performed a second time, after the British Consul had taken the couple's oaths on his diary instead of the Bible[9]. Lester was best man and made a zany film of the wedding, in which the action was speeded up and slowed down. The ceremony was also witnessed by twenty-year-old Gabrielle's father, Bernard, a Naval surgeon from Kent. Crawford registered his name as 'Michael Patrick Smith' and his job as 'photographer'. He did not record the name of his father[10].

Five months later, the Crawfords' first daughter, Emma, was born. Those early days of marriage were lived modestly in a one-bedroom flat in Clapham, South London. Each night they would turn off the mains water supply and Emma would sleep in the bath.

Another daughter, Lucy, was born in December 1967. 'I remember watching *Softly, Softly* and timing the contractions with a stopwatch,' recalled Crawford[11], who was at his wife's hospital bedside. 'They got down to forty-five-second intervals, and I asked Gabrielle if she'd mind not giving birth until the end of the episode, but she told me to find a nurse – fast. I ran off through the hospital looking for someone. But, when I finally found a nurse, I couldn't remember where Gabrielle's room was. We had to check the records.'

Crawford's 'secret' daughter made newspaper headlines when a battle over maintenance payments reached court in 1969. The actor had never denied paternity and agreed to pay £2 10s a week. A magistrate ordered this to be increased to £15, but Crawford appealed and it was halved.

At the appeal, Patricia Mansell – who claimed that he had promised to marry her – said, 'When I became pregnant, his attitude towards me changed. He didn't want to get married.' Shortly afterwards, she brought a breach of promise action against Crawford, but it was settled out of court. He paid her a lump sum[12] and set up a trust fund for daughter Angelique. In return, she and her family agreed never to discuss the matter publicly.

Chapter 7

BLACK COMEDIES

Emma Jane Crawford was born in May 1966 while her father was on stage in *The Anniversary*, a new play by Bill Mac-Ilwraith at the Duke of York's Theatre, in London's West End. One of the actor's co-stars, James Cossins, recalled 'a white and shaking Michael' during that evening's performance and 'several of us being bundled into a car afterwards to visit Gabrielle and the newly born daughter at a clinic in the Harley Street area'[1].

Crawford and Cossins were brothers Tom and Henry in the play. With brother Terry and his wife Karen, played by Jack Hedley and Sheila Hancock, they finally rebel against their fiendish mother – a wonderful performance by Mona Washbourne – who has assembled them to commemorate the anniversary of her and her late husband's wedding. June Ritchie, who had appeared alongside Crawford in *The Importance of Being Earnest* in Nottingham, here played his pregnant fiancée, Shirley, who almost has a miscarriage when Mum leaves her glass eye on the pillow of the girl's bed.

The Anniversary ran for four months and received wide acclaim. 'The play is a farce,' wrote *The Times*'s critic[2], 'but it openly exposes the violent hatreds, frustrations, and revenges which in normal farce are buried well beneath the surface. This does not stop the play from being brilliantly funny: but it is comedy that appeals to one's taste for cruelty, a form of dramatic pugilism.'

Of Mona Washbourne's central performance, *Punch* wrote, 'She hag-rides her three grown sons – a dreamy transvestite (James Cossins), stammering Jack Hedley and Michael Crawford's adenoidal Tom. To keep them with her she will employ any ruse, any lie, however foul. The play is nothing more than a succession of her venomous attacks on the sons' girls and the sons' unbelievably feeble attempts to fight back. It is well acted and well directed by Patrick Dromgoole and if you want three acts of vicious infighting, grisly humour, sadism, transvestism and incest this play contains them all.'[3]

Harold Hobson wrote in *The Sunday Times*, 'It is quite extraordinarily well acted, and Patrick Dromgoole's direction swallows its melodrama without the slightest sign of indigestion. It is to the credit of these players (and to William MacIlwraith's also) that I do not recall ever having laughed so much and so heartily at a play that I liked so little.'[4]

The birth of Crawford's daughter Emma was not the only distraction during the stage run of *The Anniversary*. That year saw England's famous World Cup victory, and James Cossins recalled 'the difficulty of getting us all out of the wardrobe at the Duke of York's – the only room with a TV set – in time for curtain up on the second house on the Saturday night that England won, and the fact that the cast were almost too hoarse to get to the end of the play'[5].

Two years later, a film version of *The Anniversary* was released, starring Bette Davis in the Mona Washbourne role of Mum. James Cossins, Jack Hedley and Sheila Hancock all appeared in it, but there was no Crawford, who was committed to other film work.

While appearing on stage in *The Anniversary*, Crawford made a new film, *The Jokers*, in which he starred with Oliver Reed. This left him very little time to sleep during the nine-week schedule. It was thought that he would be able to rest better during the day when the unit switched to night shooting, but daughter Emma – only a few weeks old – had other ideas.

The Jokers, directed by Michael Winner, was about two failed brothers who plan to steal the Crown Jewels, just to prove how easy it is, and deflate upper-class pomposity and the Establishment. First, they practise by planting small bombs around London and keeping the police on the run, then they go for their real goal, breaking into the Tower of London and burying the treasures. Beforehand, they leave letters with certain people, telling of their plan to test security. When the police catch up with them, the jewels have mysteriously disappeared and David, played by Reed, is put in jail. Crawford's character, the younger brother Michael, denies all knowledge and has an alibi. Eventually, the jewels turn up – in the Scales of Justice, over the Old Bailey.

Michael Winner, on whose original story *Likely Lads* TV writers Dick Clement and Ian La Frenais based their script, had discovered, while studying at Cambridge University, a legal loophole that meant that 'borrowing' bicycles from his college to get to the office of the student newspaper *Varsity*, which he edited, did not constitute theft, although he was gated and sent down for two weeks.[6] Using this same loophole in *The Jokers* prevented the brothers from being charged.

The Jokers proved to be Winner's first hit film, although he had received favourable American reviews for *The System*, a story of young hooligans at a British seaside resort, which also starred Oliver Reed. *The Jokers* said much about Sixties London, still swinging but not at the pace depicted by the media. Winner's aim was to reveal the truth of a society becoming richer but less happy. The brothers intend to show that they will not conform to the practices and hypocrisies of high society. David is a failed architect and Michael has been thrown out of Sandhurst where he was training for the Army. Their planting of small bombs, so that they can monitor security procedures, is followed by police and Army blundering, which was intended by Winner as a dig at Services mentality.

Crawford said at the time that he identified with his character because he felt that the enthusiasm and initiative of youth was often undervalued by the older generation.

The film was shot at some of London's top tourist landmarks, including the Tower of London and the Stock Exchange. Winner preferred to film completely on location, rather than in studios. 'Life takes place in streets, towns and not in studio mock-ups,' he said[7]. 'On location, I – and, indeed, the cameras – can get an intuitive feel of a place. I shot a scene on the top of the Old Bailey that everybody thought I could never do. We asked and got permission.'

A scene filmed in the Stock Exchange resulted in mayhem among the pinstriped brokers. The idea was to show Crawford making a phone call to warn police that a bomb was planted there. As Crawford, Winner and the ten-person film unit prepared to start work in the War Memorial Gallery, not exactly blending in with the surroundings, those on the floor of the Stock Exchange looked up, started screaming and shouting, and threw paper darts. Winner kept the powerful lights on and the cameras rolling.

The next problem was to bring in a small phone box. 'Between the stairs to the gallery, we had to cross the floor by about ten feet,' said Winner[8]. 'As it was being carried, some stockbrokers began tugging at it and a scuffle ensued. They were shouting: "You can't bring that in. Take it away – get out." I thought: "Surely no one is going to risk a fight here, of all places." Finally, we got the box – just a phone and a stand – upstairs out of their reach and continued shooting. We had to work with the gallery festooned in paper.'

Amid cries of 'Get your hair cut' and 'Go away', an unnerved Crawford told Winner, 'I can't act. I can't act with all this going on.'[9] Fortunately Winner managed to calm him down. The scene was eventually filmed after the Stock Exchange closed, at 3.30 p.m. 'We never dreamed it would cause so much fuss,' said Winner[10]. 'The London Stock Exchange turned into a complete menagerie for an hour. Here, the leaders of commerce stopped to throw paper at a film unit – like a lot of overgrown schoolboys.'

Eating out while filming on location was something Oliver Reed remembered well. 'Michael had very short arms and very long pockets,' he said[11] 'Whenever Winner and I would suggest going out to lunch, Michael would turn up late and leave early. I would put vodka in his beer, and that gave him a very grumpy constitution after lunch and he would start shouting back at Winner. Michael is a very kind person and that was against his nature, but Winner cottoned on.'

Practical jokes were the order of the day during the making of *The Jokers*; everyone played them on each other. Winner used a megaphone to relay instructions while filming, and Crawford and Reed decided to smear shoe polish round the mouthpiece, which made him look as though he was wearing black lipstick. Throwing Winner's expensive sunglasses under a bus was another jolly jape.

Reed continued the pranks when he visited Crawford at home. 'Michael is the kind of fellow who always jumps to the ready conclusion,' he said[12]. 'I would go round to his flat in Clapham when his wife's parents were there and say: "I've got the horse shit. Where can I put it?" He would go into hysterics because be believed it. Later, when he was in Wimbledon, I used to go round and drop some seeds on the ground and tell him they were pot. He would go into hysterics again, saying he had children in his house and what if the police came? They were simply forget-me-knot seeds, but he didn't know that.'

Crawford's style of acting remained indelible in his co-star's memory. 'Michael would get into Rolls-Royces by leaping across the pavement and jumping in head first,' recalled Reed[13]. 'He is small of stature and, like a small fellow who throws himself around on the rugby field, he brings out his natural aggression through falling off things and doing stunts. He's a very hard worker and very brave.'

When *The Jokers* was released, in 1967, it met with praise on both sides of the Atlantic. At the time, Crawford was appearing on Broadway in *Black Comedy*. James Powers wrote in *The Hollywood Reporter*, 'Crawford, currently starring in a New York hit play, is a new type for movies, but one that young people particularly respond to; good-natured, detached, ready for almost any lark, without thought of consequence. That at least is the role he plays and it sums up much of his generation.'[14]

Another American publication, *Time* magazine, commented, 'The only theft that comes off is Michael Crawford's – and he steals the show. Crawford, at 24, displays a plastic face and an elastic grace – comic credentials that should allow him to travel in faster and funnier company.'[15]

Many critics remarked on the rapport between the two stars. 'The lean-line droopiness of Michael Crawford and Oliver Reed's big-drum bravado make them the best double act since Laurel and Hardy,' wrote Alexander Walker in the London *Evening Standard*.[16]

The film was an undoubted success and was enhanced in America by Crawford's acclaimed Broadway performance. Before he took the trip to America, he had another film to make, during one of the most prolific periods of his career.

He also returned to television, with two ITV plays, the first of which was *The Move After Checkmate*. It was a thriller starring Donald Pleasence and Peter Vaughan, and was made at Anglia TV's Norwich studios and on location in London. Crawford played a gangland boss's son who was used by police as a means of getting his father to confess to unsolved crimes. The play, by Barry England, also included in its cast two of Crawford's colleagues from repertory theatre days, Alan Howard from Coventry and Ken McReddie from Nottingham.

In 1966 fewer television programmes were being broadcast live, but equipment was still not advanced enough to avoid shooting each scene in one complete go. Director Alvin Rakoff had problems with Crawford when it came to a crucial, very dramatic scene that he shared with Donald Pleasence, who was playing the police officer who could see a way to nailing the crook whom he had been trying to get for twenty years through his son. Rakoff recalled:

This scene with Pleasence and the other policeman ran between four and five minutes. It was the key scene emotionally for Michael. It went reasonably well, but it wasn't technically quite up to standard. I went down to the studio floor from the control room and Michael was very upset at having to do it again. He felt he had done it absolutely as best he could and there was no way he could repeat the emotion. Basically, he didn't want to do it again. I explained the problems and we re-did it.

As we finished the scene, Michael's whole body sagged. It was awful, terrible. He was just upset and near to tears. It was the fact that he felt he had done it right the first time and not nearly as well the second time. I went down to the floor and said to him: 'Come into the control room and I'll play you both "takes", with all their faults and imperfections. You will pick whichever tape you think is the right one and that is the tape I will cut into the final show.' He didn't believe me; he thought I was kidding. We ran it and he turned round to me and said: 'The second one is miles better.' I said: 'I hope you have learned something from this: it's difficult for you to judge for yourself; you must rely on other people; and, when *you* think it's gone wonderfully, it hasn't always.' He absolutely agreed.

Michael was a cracking young actor. I was surprised he didn't make bigger stardom long before he did. I remember hearing about him a lot earlier, when an American film producer, Hal E. Chester, said to me, around the time Michael was making *Two Left Feet*, that he had seen 'a young James Stewart called Michael Crawford' and to watch out for him.[17]

The feelings of Sixties youth had been at the centre of Crawford's most successful screen characters, but his third film with director Richard Lester was to incense the older generation in a way that no film had done before. *How I Won the War* was Lester's first 'serious' film, not only an anti-war film but an attack on war films themselves.

After *The Anniversary*'s stage run finished, Crawford prepared for filming in West Germany and Spain. Jack Hedley and James Cossins, who had acted his brothers in the play, were now cast in *How I Won the War*, as was Sheila Hancock, who had played his sister-in-law. Beatle John Lennon was also featured and the supporting cast included Roy Kinnear, Sir Michael Hordern and Robert Hardy.

Crawford played Lieutenant Ernest Goodbody, a British Army officer during the Second World War who, through his ineptitude, kills off, one by one, all members of his unit. The significant event is the landing of Goodbody's patrol behind enemy lines in North Africa, where they set up an 'advanced-area cricket pitch', for the purpose of 'morale' and to impress a visiting military VIP as 'a small patch of sanity'. Goodbody is captain and chief bowler of his team; the opposition – with Hitler as scorer – are 569 for no wicket. This is an allegory for the officer's bungling incompetence.

'At about the time we finished making *The Knack*,' said Richard Lester[18], 'I bought the book of *How I Won the War*, by Patrick Ryan, and started work with Charles Wood on a screenplay, with Michael in mind as the lead. It took us seven drafts before we got what we wanted, before we felt it worked. It was a piece we felt very strongly about and was very complicated.

'Primarily, it was attacking that extraordinary wave of nostalgia that seemed to occur in the early and mid-Sixties for how great it was in the war. Montgomery at the time was wandering around with a BBC camera crew all across Africa, talking about his ability. The film was a reaction against that, the delusion that nostalgia brings to something that was thoroughly horrible.'

Lester remembered the filming as 'very hard work', but much excitement was had by the cast on location, first in West Germany, where the British Army on the Rhine's tanks were used, then in Spain, where the North African scenes were shot. James Cossins recalled 'the fun of the supper parties after filming all day in the baking heat of the sand dunes around Almeria, and the joy that ensued when, after a suitable amount of alcohol, dear Roy Kinnear could be persuaded to do his celebrated impression of a one-armed golfer'[19].

Crawford and his wife Gabrielle shared a villa with John and Cynthia Lennon, and they became the best of friends. It was Lennon's first straight acting role and was coolly received, but it provided another vehicle for promoting his vision of a world free of war and nuclear weapons. Crawford recalled of Lennon, 'He'd come in and sit cross-legged on the bed with his guitar or we'd take his Rolls to the beach.'[20] It was while in Spain that Lennon wrote the Beatles classic 'Strawberry Fields Forever'.

Lester was producing for the first time, after his experience with *A Funny Thing Happened On the Way To the Forum*. Director of photography David Watkin, who had worked with Lester on *The Knack*, remembered with trepidation one of the stunts Crawford insisted on doing in this new film. 'Michael has a great determination to do everything himself and get it right,' said Watkin[21]. 'There was a scene where his unit came across a camp of German soldiers who were doing press-ups. Michael was looking over the top of a cliff at them and had to fall over, hanging in mid-air. We would usually let a stuntman do that.' A safety harness was used, but the stunt was still daring.

Crawford described *How I Won the War* as 'a brilliant movie'[22], but reviews were mixed, partly depending on each critic's political opinions. Penelope Mortimer wrote in *The Observer*, 'Lieutenant Ernest Goodbody – brilliantly played by Michael Crawford – is the prototype silly ass. For the first time – and it's about time – we see Bertie Wooster as he really is, a bungling destroyer of sensibility, eagerly and inanely driving his men on to set up an advanced cricket pitch 100 miles behind enemy lines.'[23]

In America the film trade paper *Variety* called the picture 'an uneven, forced black comedy in which liabilities outweigh assets'[24]. *Films In Review* insisted it was 'a disgusting example of the nastiness that has recently become part of the nihilism promoted by those films which are put together by Britain's mod-monsters (infantile leftists, smarty-pant degenerates, jungle-&-junkie-headed rock-n-folkers, addled well-meaners et al)'[25].

Perhaps the dilemmas of making such a film were best summed

up by William Johnson in *Film Quarterly*. 'Despite its many flaws of conception and execution,' he wrote[26], '*How I Won the War* is still the nearest thing to an effective antiwar film that I've yet seen. But I wonder whether nearest is near enough.'

For Lester, the film was one of his most satisfying. He said:

I felt very positive about it and that it was coming out the way we hoped it would. I packed in a lot of the things I wanted to and felt we had achieved what we set out to do. That doesn't mean it necessarily worked or was good; but, once the script is settled in your mind, the best you can hope for is that the finished film reflects those ambitions. It might be that your ambitions are seriously flawed and you are preaching only to the converted. You might be alienating a lot of the audience you are trying to reach.

What I remember most about *How I Won the War* was the difficulty in trying to make the nuances work in other countries. One of the major qualities of Michael's performance was that he had to speak in three accents: one way to his troops, as their superior; another way to the officers, his superiors; and a third way to the German who had captured him. The relationships of class in England were encapsulated in Michael's change of accent. In Germany, where it was dubbed into the native language, it made no sense whatsoever.

In America, the problem came with one of the more interesting surrealist ideas. As each person dies, he does so in a little skirmish of the platoon that is parallel to, and reflects, one of the four major disastrous battles of the war – Dunkirk, Dieppe, Alamein and Arnhem – which is shown in tinted black-and-white footage, some of which we shot and some of it archive material. Out of each battle, when the person dies, his replacement – his ghost – appears in the same tinted colour and keeps the unit up to complement. In America, they made six hundred prints of the film and decided these bits were supposed to be in black-and-white and they could fix it! I arrived for the American première and these ghosts made no sense at all.[27]

During filming in Spain, there had already been a hint of what was to come when a journalist heard about this 'controversial' picture being made and managed to steal a script from the set, escaping by throwing beer glasses at cast and crew. His story was not used in any British newspapers, but the real backlash came when *How I Won the War* was screened at the Pavilion Cinema in London's West End, in October 1967, exactly twenty-five years after the battle of El Alamein, which saw the war begin to swing in Britain's favour. Punches were exchanged in the centre aisle of the cinema and twenty demonstrators were escorted out by police, although no arrests were made. The film had to be stopped for seven minutes, during which one man shouted through a loud-hailer, 'We, the National Front, protest against this anti-British rubbish, especially at the time of El Alamein.'[28] One demonstrator described the film as 'an obscene insult to our war dead'[29].

Crawford was quick to respond. 'I am very proud of what the film has said – and by saying this I could possibly lose a lot of work from the people who make glamorous war films,' he admitted[30]. 'I am not worried by this because I do believe war has been glamorised beyond all belief.' Of Britain's involvement in the Second World War, he said, 'We had to fight, of course we had to fight. I think it's fine to remember – and we bloody well should remember – the people that died for us and the people who are maimed and around the twist because of it. Do you think they want to go through it again? I have an uncle who was a prisoner in a Japanese war camp. He wouldn't dream of talking about the war. He can't – he wakes up sobbing in the middle of the night.' At this time, there was no mention of his mother's first husband.

During a period when Crawford was moving swiftly between film, television and theatre, he jumped at the chance to act on the American stage for the first time. He was offered a starring role in Liverpool-born playwright Peter Shaffer's *Black Comedy*. It had already been performed in Britain and was due to open in Boston, then on Broadway as the second part of a double-bill, with another of Shaffer's one-act plays, *White Lies*.

Crawford travelled to New York by himself and booked into the Algonquin Hotel just before Christmas 1966, tucking into a turkey sandwich and cold tea on the festive day and desperately missing wife Gabrielle and baby Emma, who were staying with Gabrielle's father on his farm in Kent. Crawford went to two Christmas parties, where nobody spoke to him and he didn't like the food. To add to his misery, the television set in his hotel room did not work and he spent thousands of dollars on transatlantic telephone calls.

Gabrielle and Emma arrived in time to see Crawford open in Boston, alongside Lynn Redgrave and Geraldine Page. After Boston, they moved into Sir John Gielgud's New York apartment, in Central Park West. Once settled in, Crawford established a routine of returning from each night's performances at the Ethel Barrymore Theater and sitting on the floor eating English food, drinking orange squash out of Woolworth glasses and playing Monopoly[31].

On stage, *White Lies* was the curtain-raiser and Crawford played a sad fellow called Tom, which rather depressed him. His love affair was with laughter, and it came in *Black Comedy* when his character, sculptor Brindsley Miller, was improving the look of his shabby flat by 'borrowing' priceless porcelain and antique furniture from his friend next door to impress his fiancée's snooty father, who is visiting on the same evening that the supposed richest man in the world is arriving to inspect his sculpture. When Brindsley has to return everything, the lights fuse and the comedy begins. 'I have to move furniture to lines,' Crawford said at the time[32]. 'If a sigh is four beats too late, I'm on the other side of the stage four beats too early and the laugh is dead and I've lost one of the best moments in the show.'

The Broadway opening was cancelled because of a blizzard. When the big night finally arrived, New York's all-powerful theatre critics raved about the acting performances, but the play soon became, literally, a pain in the neck for its star.

'One night during my routine,' he recalled[33], 'we mistimed a scene in which the door slammed in my face as I was about to walk through it. It caught me smack in the forehead and knocked me back three feet. It got the biggest laugh of the night, so we decided to keep it in. So, night after night for six months, I had this door banged against my head.'

The result was a whiplash neck that required him to wear a brace between performances and did not heal completely for three years. Crawford's willingness to suffer for the good of the show, beyond the call of duty, was an early example of the masochistic rigours he would endure for the sake of comedy. 'I wouldn't give up those laughs for anything,' he told *Time* magazine[34]. 'My injuries are pleasure bumps.'

There were plenty of pleasure bumps. He also suffered a gashed and infected back, four ankle sprains, torn ligaments and splinters in all ten fingers as a result of his athleticism in the show, which included crashing to the floor entangled in telephone wire and skidding down a staircase on his heel. Walter Kerr wrote in the *New York Times*, 'He deserves a Tony, if not the Nobel, for expertise in a special nose-bashing category, which will have to be created for him alone.'[35] He added, 'The sight gags are fast, and they keep the line gags from having to work too hard. Your joy in the exercise will depend upon the depth of your appetite for more and more of the same. I got about halfway, and then wished for a spurt of invention that *didn't* depend upon one strident clown shaking a furious finger at someone who was standing two feet behind him.'

Other critics who could not get worked up about the play also admired the acting. 'The dialogue is thin, the mistaken identities predictable,' wrote Mel Gussow in *Newsweek* magazine[36]. 'It is not truth that comes out of the *Black Comedy*'s darkness, but only sight gags. *White Lies* ... in contrast, is about lying in the daylight. In Baroness Lemberg's creepily ornate fortunetelling parlor the lights are on and the baroness (Miss Page) is supposedly tuned in to the truth. But everyone lies. There are too few surprises in this one. In both plays the actors are fine and resourceful. It is the playwright who apparently ran short of ideas.'

Crawford was a British star on Broadway and, for his considerable pains, won two Best Actor honours, the *Variety* Critics' Award and the Whitbread Anglo-American Group Award. He also found a different sort of fame through his increasing interest in photography, when *Life* magazine commissioned him to take pictures of the wedding of his co-star Lynn Redgrave – who played his fiancée in *Black Comedy* – to producer-director John Clark in April 1967.

After his lonely first days in America, Crawford was soon in demand socially, and it was Gabrielle's turn to be lonely. 'Michael had a lot of lunches, and in New York they tend to ask a man on his own,' she said[37]. 'We didn't have an unlimited budget and, after the first few weeks, the shops stopped being interesting. I used to take my daughter, Emma, to children's parties and I wandered around Central Park quite a lot. But, if you asked me what I did during those months, I couldn't come up with anything constructive.'

Another dark side to Crawford's starring role on Broadway was a picket by American actors outside shows with British cast members. 'I'm black and blue from head to toe,' said Crawford then[38], 'I've got eight pulled ligaments in my leg and bruises all over and, when I limp out of the theatre at night, these bloody bastards are walking up and down with signs saying "English actors will be working next year – will you?". It's depressing to feel you're not wanted here.'

Slightly more diplomatically, he said, 'I sympathize. American actors in England should be given the same rights we're given here. You can't do all plays there with strictly British actors. But how many of those blokes carrying signs outside *Black Comedy* can take the falls I do eight times a week? After each show I want to come outside and hit those guys in the nose. The problem should be resolved by British and American unions over conference tables. I'm paying seventy-five dollars a week to American Actors' Equity just for the privilege of acting on stage here. What Americans pay in England is nothing compared to that.'[39]

Politics aside, Crawford's black-and-blue comedy had made him a star with New York theatre-goers, and the American film industry was about to capitalize on this young star who would do anything.

Chapter 8

HELLO, DOLLY!

During the 1967 San Francisco Film Festival, Crawford met Gene Kelly, the song-and-dance maestro who had himself been a hit on the Broadway stage before starring in film musicals such as *Singing In the Rain*. Now Kelly was planning to direct a film version of *Hello, Dolly!*, whose associate producer, Roger Edens, had seen Crawford in *Black Comedy* and in the film *The Jokers*. Edens phoned producer Ernest Lehman and said, 'I've found the boy to play Cornelius.'[1] Cornelius Hackl was the naive young chief clerk of the musical's hay and feed store. Lehman thought that Crawford might be too young, but Gene Kelly decided to see him.

Crawford travelled to San Francisco for two days with director Richard Lester to see a screening of *How I Won the War*. At his hotel, there was a message, 'Gene Kelly called and will be in later.' He rushed up to his room and changed, then sat around wondering whether he looked right. He had a shower and changed, then had another shower and changed again. The doorbell rang and he was caught between changes, opening the door with just a towel wrapped around him.

'Can you sing?' asked Kelly. 'Sure,' replied Crawford. 'I used to be an opera singer.' 'Can you dance?' 'Well, I've done a bit in the bath.' Kelly smiled. 'I used to love your pictures with Ginger Rogers,' said Crawford lightheartedly, momentarily confusing the star with Fred Astaire. Kelly just smiled again.

'Let's see you do this,' said Kelly, launching into a routine around the hotel suite. 'But I've only just got off the plane,' insisted

Crawford. 'I haven't had any breakfast yet and I get dizzy if I start moving my feet fast before I've eaten.'

Kelly grinned. 'When you've had some breakfast, make a film test,' he said. 'What we want is someone who's an idiot and who has appeal. My wife thinks you've got appeal and I think you're a bit of an idiot.'

Crawford jumped at the chance to star alongside Barbra Streisand and Walter Matthau in a Hollywood musical, having just turned down £10,000 to appear in a British film. 'I wouldn't do it,' he said[2], 'because it was another anti-war film and I wanted something with some fun in it.' *Hello, Dolly!* also had money in it, reputedly paying him £100,000, and more for just the rehearsals than his total previous showbusiness earnings.

Back in Britain, Crawford found himself a choreographer, Leo Charibean, who taught him to dance the American way. He practised day and night, then went to St John's Wood Studios, in North London, with David Watkin – who filmed *The Knack* and *How I Won the War* – to record a screen test in a day. Within six hours of the short film arriving at Twentieth Century-Fox's studios in America, Crawford received a telephone call to say he had the part. 'Not only that,' recalled Crawford[3]. 'They thought that what we had done was an example of how a test should be made. Richard Zanuck, vice-president of Twentieth Century-Fox, said it was the best he had seen.' It took another two months for the contract to be drawn up.

The story of *Hello, Dolly!* had a long history. It started as *A Day Well Spent*, a British play by John Oxenford, performed in London in 1835, before being adapted by a Viennese playwright, Johann Nestroy, into *Einen Jux Will er Sich Machien* ('He Wants To Have a Lark'), staged in Austria in 1842. Almost a hundred years later, the great American dramatist Thornton Wilder turned it into *The Merchant of Yonkers* and later revised it, changing the name to *The Matchmaker*. This stage version was directed in Britain by Sir Tyrone Guthrie and performed at the Edinburgh Festival and in London in 1954. Some of the cast transferred to the Broadway production the following year, but none appeared in the 1958 film version, also called *The Matchmaker*, which featured Shirley Mac-Laine alongside Shirley Booth. In 1964, it was turned into a stage musical under the title *Hello, Dolly!*, with Carol Channing in the lead role. It ran on Broadway for 2,844 performances and won nine Tony Awards.

Fired by the success of its 1965 Rodgers and Hammerstein musical, *The Sound of Music*, Twentieth Century-Fox paid $2,500,000 for the film rights. The deal also included provisions for royalties to be paid on box-office takings and a guarantee that the film would not be released before the stage show closed or 20 June 1971, whichever was the earlier. Richard Zanuck assigned the production and screenplay to Ernest Lehman, who had written *North by Northwest* and *The Sound of Music*.

The first mistake was the miscasting of Barbra Streisand in the lead role of Dolly Levi. Streisand, at twenty-five when filming began, was too young for the role. Although experienced on stage and television, she had made only one film, *Funny Girl*, unreleased then but set to win her an Oscar. Clearly she was a major talent, but she was simply wrong for *Hello, Dolly!*

'We wanted Carol Channing,' said Ernest Lehman[4], 'but the trouble was Carol didn't photograph too well; it had nothing to do with the fact that she wasn't as big a marquee name as Streisand. Frankly, I would have preferred Carol to Barbra. But, after seeing *Thoroughly Modern Millie*, I honestly felt that I couldn't take a whole movie in which Carol was in practically every scene. Her personality is just too much for the cameras to contain.'

Channing had spent almost four years in the stage role, which also provided late-career hits for Ginger Rogers and Betty Grable, who were no longer considered box-office attractions. Lehman also ruled out Elizabeth Taylor, who had starred in *Who's Afraid of Virginia Woolf?*, which he wrote and produced, and who wanted the role of Dolly. *The Sound of Music* star Julie Andrews was also considered, but Lehman thought she would be totally wrong. By this time, he believed there were no suitable 'mature' actresses left, so he looked for someone with the necessary vocal ability. Streisand was hired for a reported $750,000, plus a percentage of box-office takings.

Next, Gene Kelly was engaged as director, because of his wide experience in musicals. Initially he was unsure about accepting the job. 'I was a bit worried about taking a show that has been one of the great musical hits of all time, which I felt was a bit of fluff with one big smash song,' he said[5]. 'I was quite worried about making it hold up on the screen for two-and-a-half hours and it gave me pause. Then, my curiosity and the challenge took over and I accepted the job.'

The $24,000,000 production was to be an unmitigated disaster and was to bring Twentieth Century-Fox close to bankruptcy when it found out that the heyday of the film musical was past.

In January 1968 Crawford and his family, which now included baby Lucy, set off for six months in Hollywood. The thought of playing No 3 in the cast, alongside Streisand and Walter Matthau, terrified the British star. 'But then I found out all the others were too – Barbra Streisand and Gene Kelly, the director,' he said[6].

Arriving in Hollywood was also daunting for Gabrielle. 'At first, it was very glamorous,' she recalled almost twenty years later[7]. 'There was dinner with Julie Christie and swimming with Gene Kelly. These were the kind of people I had pinned up on my bedroom wall, and here I was meeting them. I was twenty-one at the time and the whole experience gave me a lot of confidence.'

But soon she experienced the misery of the lonely wife, staying at a Bel Air mansion, coping with two babies and playing tennis when she could to fill the void. She took up tennis after finding that she was simply in the way if she appeared on the film set. 'Michael's not the sort of person who wants you to be around all the time,' she said[8]. 'He's very independent and, although I used to read his scripts, I soon discovered Michael needs to be alone to work. The support he needed wasn't somebody standing next to him.' After little more than two years of marriage, Gabrielle's experience was a hint of what was to come.

Crawford and the rest of the cast began rehearsals with Gene Kelly and choreographer Michael Kidd in February 1968, and they began the ninety-day shoot on 15 April. On the set, the legendary feuds between Barbra Streisand and Walter Matthau were hotting up. Matthau played Horace Vandergelder, the wealthy 'hay and feed' merchant from Yonkers on whom Dolly sets her sights as a second husband. But there was no love lost between the stars. Tempers reached breaking point when filming moved to the New York locations, where it was hot and muggy. On the June day when American presidential candidate Robert Kennedy was assassinated, emotions were high and Matthau exploded.

'As if contending with the elements were not enough,' Matthau recalled[9], 'Barbra kept asking Gene whether he didn't think it would be better if I did this on this line, and that on the other, etc, etc – and I told her to stop directing the fucking picture ... I'm not the most diplomatic man in the world, and we began a slanging match like a couple of kids from the ghetto.'

Gene Kelly forced the stars to agree a truce, but their relationship only worsened. The director put their problems down to Streisand's insecurity. 'If only there'd been more time,' said Kelly[10], 'I'd have tried to help her work out a clear-cut characterisation, but we had a tight schedule and I left it up to her.'

Crawford's own relations with Streisand were happy. 'I really loved her,' he recalled[11], 'not only because she looked beautiful, but because she's basic and natural. She can't stand idiots and inefficiency; nor can I. So that was a bond between us. Mind you, she asks a lot of questions which tend to drive you insane when you want to get on with the job, and sometimes I used words not heard in the best society. "Gee," she used to say, "his language is bad." But we never had any genuine arguments.'

Throughout shooting, Crawford was on the set all the time, even when not needed, because it was his first film musical and he was eager to learn. 'Most of the sequences went well,' he said[12]. 'And apart from Barbra arriving late – which she wouldn't have done had she only been given one hairdresser instead of three, because all three insisted on fixing her hair, and that took time – everything went smoothly.'

Putting aside the personal feud between Streisand and Matthau, Crawford considered the one 'destructive element' in the production to be Ernest Lehman, who walked around looking unhappy throughout. 'But, then, anything Ernest does is bound to make him unhappy,' said Crawford[13]. 'He's that sort of person. Now, with Gene it's just the reverse. He brings a joy and an ebullience to his work which is a fantastic morale booster for the cast. Nothing is too much trouble or effort for him. There were some weekends when he would phone me up and ask if he could come round because he'd thought of something new for me to do, and he'd jump into his car and come all the way just to give me a new inflection on a word!'

Overall, making *Hello, Dolly!* and working with Kelly was a profitable experience for Crawford. 'I would never have been a dancer or believed I could do anything if it had not been for him,' said Crawford[14]. 'He helped and encouraged me so much.'

Crawford's big production number, *It Only Takes a Moment*, came during the film's last half-hour, as Cornelius Hackl declares his love for Irene Molloy, played by Marianne McAndrew. It was the song that Crawford's singing teacher had prepared him well for, and the star put all his emotion into it. 'By the end of the shot I was crying,' he said after finishing the film[15]. 'I've seen the "rushes" and I look hideous – it isn't glamorous when you're really crying. Your mouth goes hard and ugly as you try to choke back the tears, but it is honest.'

The film itself was a massive investment for Twentieth Century-Fox. The New York street in which much of the action took place was a Hollywood studio set costing more than two million dollars, the most expensive ever constructed. It consisted of a complex of sixty buildings, with reproductions of intersections of Manhattan's Fifth Avenue, Broadway and Mulberry Street, and subsections for Madison Square Park, 14th Street and the Bowery. The costumes were stunning, and choreographer Michael Kidd completely restaged the dance sequences.

By February 1969, *Hello, Dolly!* was ready for screening, but the Broadway production was still running and it looked as if it might be more than two years before the film could be shown. Twentieth Century-Fox, desperate to recoup its investment, negotiated a new deal with David Merrick, producer of the stage show. Studio head Richard Zanuck paid him between one and two million dollars so that the film could be released that year, with a guarantee to compensate him if the show's gross takings fell below $60,000 a week for an agreed period.

Crawford attended the world première of *Hello, Dolly!*, at the Rivoli Theater, New York, on 16 December and, for a while, it looked as if Twentieth Century-Fox's gamble might have paid off. However, after a few weeks, cinema audiences dropped dramatically and the moment of truth arrived. The film studio had already seen two of its other musical extravaganzas, *Doctor Dolittle* and *Star!*, flop as people shied away from this type of entertainment and cinemas began to show harder, more permissive productions aimed at young people.

American reviews were mixed. Crawford's performance also

met with a mixed reception. *Variety* wrote, 'Though an actor since age 13, Crawford had never before danced and he is surprisingly successful at it, in some measure due to Gene Kelly having personally helped him weekends during the shooting.'[16]

Motion Picture Herald described him as 'just too, too coy'[17] and *The Hollywood Reporter* wrote, 'As the overaged adolescent clerk, Michael Crawford contrives a high pitched American accent that soon strains, particularly under the constant reminders that he is 28¾-years-old. A respectable attempt at comic characterization, its undiminished contrivance ultimately mars the simplicity of *It Only Takes a Moment*, already performed as a send-up of movie love balladry, with townspeople and extras wandering in for the chorus.'[18]

The British release followed shortly afterwards. It was generally well received by critics, but there were a few dissenting voices. 'Darling Dolly should raise the spirits of everyone connected with the film industry, from tycoons to tea boys,' declared Marjorie Bilbow in the trade publication *Today's Cinema*[19]. 'Ask not for whom the box-office till rings: it rings for all when the missing millions creep out of their burrows to find enchantment waiting for them.'

Kinematograph Weekly was equally enthusiastic: 'With familiar and popular songs, brilliant dancing, colourful period decor and, of course, Barbra Streisand, there is little chance of this being anything but a big success.'[20]

Films and Filming compared the stars with those in the 1958 non-musical screen version. 'Nobody in the present cast is in the race,' wrote Gordon Gow[21], 'with the single exception of Walter Matthau who deadpans beautifully as the miser Vandergelder and even gets away with his preposterous *volte-face* in the telescoped conclusion.'

The *Daily Mirror* conceded that the story was 'still corny, predictable and thin to the point of malnutrition' but believed that the lavish settings, its song-and-dance routines and the cast made up for this and added that Crawford 'brings a superb youthful energy to the role of the gawky, naive young clerk'[22].

Perhaps the most damning criticism of Crawford's performance came years later in Donald Zec and Anthony Fowles's biography of Streisand, *Barbra*. 'Casting Britain's Michael Crawford in the role of Cornelius was close to unintended farce,' they wrote[23]. 'An amiable and versatile performer, Crawford in *Dolly* stretches his theater-bred talents beyond their limits. When, in a voice that is neither, he sings "My arms were sure and strong", a glance at his thin arms and meagre frame brings you dangerously close to a belly-laugh.'

Generally the failure of *Hello, Dolly!* did no harm to Crawford, Walter Matthau or Gene Kelly. Streisand took the flak and Twentieth Century-Fox executives braced themselves for a financial disaster. The trade publication *Variety* later estimated the film's American box-office takings at $15,000,000, creditable for most productions but a massive shortfall on its $24,000,000 investment.

Amid the gloom and doom, the American film industry rather charitably nominated *Hello, Dolly!* for seven Oscars, including one for Best Film, but there was, conspicuously, no nomination for Streisand. The film won three Oscars, for Best Art Direction, Best Scoring of a Musical and Best Sound.

The Oscars were small consolation. The ramifications of Twentieth Century-Fox's débâcle were immediate. Even before *Hello, Dolly!* went into production, Richard Zanuck had agreed with Gene Kelly and producer Frank McCarthy, who together had made *A Guide for the Married Man*, to team them up again for a screen version of the fantasy *Tom Swift and His Wizard Airship*. Kelly had plans to feature Crawford, but the studio abandoned the project, even though two million dollars had already been spent on it. As Twentieth Century-Fox began its long, ultimately successful battle for survival, there was no room for risks.

Chapter 9

GAMES PEOPLE PLAY

Crawford was already putting his energies into another film for Twentieth Century-Fox, back in Britain. In *The Games*, he was cast as British milkman Harry Hayes, who takes up athletics for a joke, is spotted by a former champion runner and ends up in an Olympic Marathon. The director was Michael Winner, who had made *The Jokers*, and to whom Crawford sent the script.

Now living in Wimbledon, in a spacious house complete with swimming pool, Crawford went into four months' training for his gruelling role, starting each day at 6.30am with a four-mile run across the common, which he built up to twelve miles. At first the result was that his lungs hurt so much that he could hardly stand up. Soon he was being coached by former long-distance runner Gordon Pirie, the film's technical adviser, who said, 'Michael's got a good physique, his co-ordination's brilliant and he has a sparkling character. He was brilliant the very first time he ran. I ran and he went on running with me all the way. He's got the spirit to be a competitive runner.'[1] During training, Crawford reached a speed of a mile in four minutes twenty seconds, a remarkable feat for a non-professional.

Crawford found his inspiration in another of the film's advisers, Jim Peters, four times holder of the Marathon world record. As a basis for his performance, Crawford studied film of Peters staggering helplessly around the track at the 1954 Empire Games in Vancouver, Canada, unable to reach the finishing line.

'I'm basing my style on Jim Peters,' Crawford said as shooting began[2]. 'He was the greatest and I'm with him every day. He has

63

total recall of his race in Canada when he was beaten in the stadium for an Empire gold medal.' Of this new skill he had acquired, Crawford added, 'It's really giddy. For years, I've been ashamed of my body. I honestly never knew I could run.'

The film also starred Stanley Baker as Crawford's coach and Ryan O'Neal – then a star of the popular TV series *Peyton Place* – Charles Aznavour and Athol Compton as his American, Czech and Australian Marathon rivals. For O'Neal, the film simply meant sharpening up on what was already a hobby, but for French actor-singer Aznavour and unknown Aborigine postman Compton the physical demands were more exacting. All came under the guidance of Gordon Pirie. Also in the film were Jeremy Kemp as the Australian's coach and Mona Washbourne, who played Crawford's mother on stage in *The Anniversary*, as his mother here.

Location shooting took place in London, Vienna, Sydney, Tokyo and, for the film's climactic scenes, Rome. At the beginning of filming, the physical exertions began to catch up with Crawford, who needed injections in his left leg, which was hurting furiously. Then, in the freezing cold of London in February 1969, his feet swelled up. Fortunately he was on form the following week for shooting at White City stadium, in West London. In the story the Czech had to beat Harry Hayes over nine miles, which he did, but Hayes still broke the six-mile European record.

Filming then moved to Rome, where the Italian Olympic Committee provided use of the Olympic stadium and offices, and helped Michael Winner to close up to six miles of streets each day so that he could shoot the Marathon. Filling the stadium was achieved by mixing a thousand real people with more than 60,000 fibreglass dummies. This was where the Marathon finished, after its long trek through the streets of Rome, taking in tourist attractions such as the Piazza Navona, one of the city's typical squares, the Trevi Fountain and the Piazzale del Faro, near the Viale Giannicolo, on one of Rome's Seven Hills, the Janiculum.

In the Piazza Navona, with its seventeenth-century buildings and three spectacular fountains, flags of different countries fluttered in the breeze, hundreds of 'extras' acted as spectators lining the route and Winner directed affairs with the use of his famous loudhailer. The race was supposed to be taking place in blazing sunshine, but the sun refused to come out and there was even some rain. When the weather improved, filming went ahead, with all mackintoshes put well out of sight.

Crawford had been ordered to take a few days' rest after pulling a leg muscle, but he was back after only a day, filming at the Piazzale del Faro. He was heard to say to Winner, 'You know, I feel that in this sequence I'm running a bit too slowly. Can't you speed it up?'[3]

To film the Marathon, Winner used eleven cameras scattered throughout Rome, to give the impression of a continuous event. The seventeen hours of film took Winner two months to edit down to fifteen minutes. As intended, it was the highlight of the film and successfully reflected the pain endured by long-distance runners. Crawford's character finishes eighth but, having overtaxed himself, he then collapses on the track. The Czech, beaten at the last moment by the Australian, is congratulated on coming second and replies, 'But I didn't win.'

Despite a weak script, the film certainly conveyed the motivation behind Marathon runners and the pain they endure in an effort to win at all costs. 'In all my films,' said Winner[4], 'the underlying theme is the individual seeking to prove himself against the mass, to set himself above the environment. The main idea of *The Games* is that to run a Marathon is a lonely and extraordinary thing to do.'

Winner had been worried about the script from the beginning. 'Fox, although allowing me complete control over the physical side of making the picture, were strong enough to prevent me changing the script,' he said[5]. 'They kept saying they thought it was a fine script, and I kept saying it wasn't. I used to go to work fearful of the dialogue I was putting on the screen. I would look at the lines and tremble. I knew it would fall flat; but it wasn't the bad script which made the film unsuccessful. People just didn't want to see a sports film.'

Film critics immediately latched on to the weak script. Marjorie Bilbow wrote in *Today's Cinema*, 'With emotional involvement spread thinly over four heroes from four nations, the story content is less than absorbing. Impressed by Michael Winner's astounding ability to create his own Olympic Games in Italy, awed by the facts and figures forming the background to this mind-boggling undertaking, I remained only fleetingly interested in the people involved.'[6]

Variety wrote, 'With the outdated polemics of director Michael Winner, the banalities of Erich Segal's adaptation of a Hugh Atkinson novel, and a rather lifeless and cardboard cast, the 20th-Fox release amounts to a dull Frank Merriwell yarn, hyped a bit to the level of high-school mentality.'[7] Despite the 'cardboard cast' jibe, it asserted that 'Aznavour, Crawford and Kemp come off best'.

Like most critics, Kevin Gough-Yates of *Films and Filming* found something to praise. 'The film has a bite which is all too frequently missing in the cinema,' he wrote[8]. 'Who, other than Michael Winner, would have the gall to stage an event starring Michael Crawford, Charles Aznavour and Ryan O'Neal, and have them all beaten by a totally unknown actor?'

The Games just made *Variety*'s famous list of Twentieth Century-Fox Top 10 disasters, weighing in at No. 10, with a $2,000,000 loss. Again, a film's flaws did little irreparable damage to Crawford, who could not be judged simply on his acting performance, but also for the energy and dedication he put into making his character real – and the fact that everyone *knew* that he was really running to professional standards.

Driving a Rolls-Royce into a swimming pool was Crawford's death-defying contribution to his next film, *Hello-Goodbye*. It was his third picture for Twentieth Century-Fox and his biggest screen disappointment, partly because he was miscast in the romantic lead. The film was intended to make a star of Twentieth Century-Fox boss Darryl F. Zanuck's latest protégé, French actress Geneviève Gilles, whose first picture it was, after her success as a model. She was lavishly dressed in costumes by Yves St Laurent of Paris and Valentino of Rome, and the film was shot in the beautiful settings of Cannes and the French Riviera, but Crawford soon realized that his co-star was no actress.

'The film crew were great, but the people you play opposite must also be good,' he said[9]. 'It's no good working with four duff actors when there's only five of you in it. It stands no chance at all – and really she was just awful!'

Events were not helped by an early change of director. After about two months' work on the picture, including four days' shooting, Ronald Neame – a veteran cinematographer, producer and director of British films – left, claiming too much interference from Zanuck. 'He was on the set a lot of the time,' recalled Neame[10]. 'As a senior director, I'm used to having complete creative authority while making a film and I found that I couldn't carry out my job in the manner to which I had become accustomed. My contract said very clearly that I had to have complete control of the making of the film, so I asked Darryl Zanuck if he would please replace me and I would give him the necessary time to find someone else.

'It turned out to be extremely good for me because within twenty-four hours of leaving I was asked to go to Hollywood and prepare *Scrooge* for Paramount Pictures. Their president, Gordon Stulberg, became president of Twentieth Century-Fox and asked me to direct *The Poseidon Adventure*, which became the company's most profitable film. When I left *Hello-Goodbye*, Darryl Zanuck had said, "You understand that you won't be working with Fox again." Two years later, I was making their most successful picture.'

Neame's replacement on *Hello-Goodbye* was Romanian-born director Jean Negulesco, an exile in America with a string of films behind him, including the Marilyn Monroe picture *How To Marry a Millionaire*.

Hello-Goodbye featured Crawford as a playboy adventurer, with a penchant for vintage cars, who falls for a baron's nymphomaniac wife, played by Gilles. She usually waves goodbye to men as casually as she greets them, but this time she is hooked. German actor Curt Jurgens took the role of her tolerant husband, who eventually falls for an American heiress.

Crawford's character, Harry England, had to be seen driving a forty-year-old Rolls-Royce convertible into the ten-feet-deep swimming pool of a château above Cannes after getting drunk. Stuntman David Watson, who with partner Joe Wadham had been responsible for spectacular scenes in films such as *Those Magnificent Men In Their Flying Machines*, was supposed to do this hair-raising sequence, but Crawford insisted on doing it himself.

Twentieth Century-Fox agreed to this but made Crawford sign a legal document making him personally responsible for any resulting injury or loss of life. 'I could see their point,' Crawford said afterwards[11]. 'With so much of the film completed, they weren't particularly keen to have one of their leading men at the bottom of the pool with his lungs full of water.'

Crawford had to drive the car into the pool, unlock his seat belt, put the gear into neutral, work four pedals that released oxygen tanks – to slow down the sinking – speak twelve lines of dialogue as the water bubbled up around his chin, somersault underwater so that, after total submersion, his kicking legs appeared first, then escape. 'What really scared me was the thought of forgetting those lines,' said Crawford[12]. 'To have blown them after all that would have been awful.'

More serious was the need to drive the car between twenty and thirty miles an hour. Going too fast would result in his jumping over the pool and crashing into the far end. Going too slow would not give the car enough momentum, resulting in it nose-diving into the water, overturning and trapping him underneath.

When David Watson was satisfied that Crawford had the co-ordination, timing and confidence to do the jump, he stood aside. Skin-divers were close at hand, ready to go into action if the stunt went disastrously wrong. As their cameras rolled, the film crew looked on anxiously while Crawford drove the Rolls up the ramp. His timing and execution were perfect, and the scene was done in one 'take'. If anything had gone wrong, there might have been no chances for another.

Crawford had given his all again, but the film was a catastrophe and, following Twentieth Century-Fox's string of aberrations, brought the Hollywood studio even closer to ruin.

'When the film opened,' recalled Crawford's wife, Gabrielle[13], 'we did our usual thing of driving at the crack of dawn to the air terminal to get the early newspapers. We just couldn't believe how bad the reviews were. Michael was absolutely shattered. Everything he does he throws his heart and soul into it and it just completely destroyed his confidence.'

Philip French wrote in *The Times*, 'Once again, the considerable talent of Michael Crawford is squandered on feeble material, and he is excusably incapable of convincing us of the irresistible attraction of an insipid newcomer called Geneviève Gilles, who delivers her lines as if reading them from the small print of an oculist's chart (from which they might well have derived). The buxom Mlle Gilles is called upon every 10 minutes to reveal her all (or three-quarters of it) and while this is no sight to be despised, she could have appeared stark-naked from beginning to end and still failed to distract our attention from the movie's essential mediocrity.'[14]

Kinematograph Weekly's critic remarked, 'The aura of wealth is everywhere except in the person of Michael Crawford, whose Harry is yet another study in his gallery of perky, slightly common heroes. He uses his talent for accenting throwaway lines and for pathos, as well as his sense of comedy, especially in the drunken farewell when he drowns a beautiful old Rolls-Royce in the Baron's swimming pool.'[15]

In America, *Motion Picture Herald* declared, 'Crawford is attractive and has the only spark of personality in the film but his forte is slapstick, and he has been unattractively handled in several scenes by director Jean Negulesco. He is allowed, among other things, a hangdog look that would poison champagne.'[16]

It was August 1970, and *Hello, Dolly!*, *The Games* and *Hello-Goodbye* had all been released during the previous nine months. The bright future predicted when Crawford had travelled to Hollywood two years earlier had turned sour. He made a television play but turned down all other offers that came his way, desperate to avoid another disaster.

The TV production was a Victorian melodrama called *The Policeman and the Cook*, again made by Anglia Television. Crawford played Constable Gough, a young policeman who is sent to a boarding-house to investigate a revenge murder by a jilted girl. It meant having his hair cut. 'I usually grow it like a sheepdog to keep me warm in winter,' he said at the time[17]. 'They took an inch off, and now I've got a shocking cold.'

By the time Crawford returned to the stage in mid-1971, he had not worked for fourteen months. 'I was offered many nasty films made by catch-penny producers to show off girls in the nude,' he said[18], 'but I wouldn't accept.' There was also talk of his playing Timothy Evans, who was hanged for murders to which his landlord John Christie later confessed, in a film to be called *The Christie Murders*, but it did not happen. At the same time, Columbia announced its own version of the story, *Ten Rillington Place*, starring Richard Attenborough and John Hurt, as Christie and Evans. Plans for a Broadway musical version of *Gulliver's Travels*, starring Crawford, also came to nothing.

'He was terrified of making another mistake,' recalled wife Gabrielle[19]. 'He was desperately unhappy, and when he's unhappy he's hell to live with. He just goes quite silent and doesn't speak for days. In the beginning, I was like a little dog following him around saying: "What's the matter?" and he'd scream at me. At first, I used to sit all huddled up and think: "I just can't bear it."'

Soon Gabrielle learned to leave him alone in his despair, and he spent more time playing darts and billiards at a Battersea pub. Determined to be as good as the regulars, he practised on his own at a pub in Balham.

Another release, for husband and wife together, was going to watch Chelsea Football Club and socializing with some of the team. One of Chelsea's star players, David Webb, was godfather to the couple's eldest daughter, Emma.

Crawford's professional frustration was exacerbated by financial ruin when he invested much of his earnings from the three Twentieth Century-Fox films with a property developer who put the cash into a public company that went bust. Years later, the London Bankruptcy Court was told that Henry Pearlberg had debts of more than £2,000,000, including £257,397 invested by 'a well known actor'. Outside the court, Pearlberg revealed that Crawford was the actor but claimed that he had invested only £60,000.

Whatever the loss, it meant that the Crawfords had nothing except their Wimbledon house and a Rolls-Royce, one luxury item they had allowed themselves. The Rolls was to come in useful when Gabrielle had an idea to get them both working. Her brother, Roger Lewis, already had a company that made gigantic floor cushions, so the three of them teamed up and opened a cushion shop in Chelsea. 'They became the rage and I was delivering them all day in the Rolls,' said Crawford[20]. 'Frankly, it was our salvation. It certainly sustained me during that dreadful time. I worked in the factory and said it was for fun; but it wasn't – I did it because I *needed* to.'

Gabrielle recalled, 'Hour after hour, he'd sit stuffing cushions. It was terrible really. He'd even sit at a machine in the factory sewing patchwork cushions with all the remnants. At one stage, I couldn't even pay a medical bill for one of the children. If we hadn't had the shop, I don't know how we could have managed.'[21]

Michael Crawford in the hit musical *Barnum*, 1981.

Crawford (centre) left school at the age of fifteen and made his screen debut in the Children's Film Foundation production *Soapbox Derby*, starring as the leader of one of two rival gangs building cars to race.

A second production for the Children's Film Foundation, *Blow Your Own Trumpet*, saw Crawford as a youngster who learns to play the cornet, then, thanks to a mischievous dog, loses his trousers while performing in a competition.

As Jaffet, Noah's eldest son, Crawford starred alongside Owen Brannigan in the
première of Benjamin Britten's *Noye's Fludde,* at the Aldeburgh Festival, in 1958.

Crawford (right) was sixteen when he, Sarah Long and Keith Crane played the juvenile leads in *Head of the Family* at the Belgrade Theatre, Coventry.

The twenty-six-part TV series *Sir Francis Drake* featured Crawford as cabin boy John Drake, the adventurer's nephew. He was recommended for the role by *Danger Man* star Patrick McGoohan, with whom Crawford had appeared in the film *Two Living, One Dead*.

Julia Foster played Crawford's girlfriend in *Two Left Feet*, a film that set the actor off on a string of accident-prone roles. It was Crawford's starring role on screen as an adult, but the film's impact was lost by a delay of more than two years in its release.

When Crawford was required to be pulled off a dock into a lake on water skis for the film *The Knack . . . and how to get it*, the experts said it could not be done. He proved them wrong on the second 'take'.

Despite having all the ingredients of a good film, *A Funny Thing Happened On the Way To the Forum* was ultimately a disappointment. Even the regular appearances of handmaidens and vestal virgins could not knit together the disparate elements.

Crawford and Oliver Reed played two brothers who 'borrow' the Crown Jewels in *The Jokers*, a film intended by director Michael Winner to highlight a British society that was becoming richer but less happy.

Spain was the location for filming the African scenes in *How I Won the War*, a controversial anti-war production that featured John Lennon (second right) alongside Crawford.

The Crawfords were living from week to week, and soon the Rolls-Royce had to go. 'We'd bought our house in Wimbledon on what I'd saved up from all my other work,' said Crawford[22], 'and then I had to start worrying about having to pay the mortgage. We didn't tell anyone. We just never talked about it. But it's times like that when you find who your friends are. With not working and not going out, the invitations stopped coming in. But what the hell. We learned an awful lot in that year. The trouble was, I was terrified to do anything else after making the mistake with *Hello-Goodbye*.' When the right job did turn up, it was relief for the frustrated star, but it also signalled the end of his marriage.

Chapter 10

NO SEX, PLEASE

When Crawford was offered the starring role in a new British stage farce, he was unsure whether to accept. 'Over the months,' recalled wife Gabrielle[1], 'he got more and more depressed and finally, when the script for *No Sex, Please – We're British* came in, I said: "You must take it. You can't sit around for ever. You're just going down and down." Finally, he said he'd do it.'

In the play, which was to tour Britain before running in London's West End, Crawford was cast as Runnicles, a bank clerk given the task of disposing of piles of pornography that is delivered to the manager and his wife. Anthony Marriott and Alistair Foot's script called for the clerk to be a 'heavy' type, but Crawford was successful in changing the underling to a meek, nervous sort. He then added his own slapstick comedy, each night diving head first through a serving hatch and generally being thrown around. Also featured in the play, as the bank manager and his wife, were Anthony Valentine and Canadian actress Linda Thorson, best known for her TV role as Tara King in *The Avengers*.

Crawford had lost so much confidence before taking on the play that he decided he must live the part and put everything into it. For the three weeks of rehearsals before the production opened in Edinburgh, he moved out of his Wimbledon home and stayed in a small hotel room, away from his wife and children. Gabrielle attended the opening night, the play toured the country – although the citizens of Eastbourne did not have the pleasure of it because the local council would not allow it to be staged unless the title was changed – and the West End beckoned.

No Sex, Please – We're British opened at the Strand Theatre on 3 June 1971, and Crawford was so nervous that he was sick off stage three times. The play itself was panned by critics, but they found much to praise in Crawford's performance. 'Most of the fun lies in the capable hands of Michael Crawford as a witless bank cashier who is deputed to de-porn the flat,' wrote the London *Evening News*[2]. 'With a forlorn expression, a pansy voice and a surprisingly athletic body Mr Crawford makes a real joy of his role, tumbling about, doing everything wrong and getting 99 per cent of the laughs.'

The Times wrote of the farce, 'It yields only one performance of any bite. This comes from Michael Crawford as the luckless cashier who couples a weedy spineless manner with a staggering display of gymnastic comedy, catching armfuls of books, left hanging by one hand from a picture frame in mid-chase, and executing a perfect dive through a kitchen hatch. The performance challenges comparison with Robert Hirsch[3].'[4]

John Barber, in the *Daily Telegraph*, described Crawford as 'a winsome young comedian who recalls Harold Lloyd' and his performance as 'a continual delight' but added, 'It should perhaps be said that there is nothing pornographic in the show – nor, I am afraid, much wit or natural jollity. But by the end, when a couple of under-dressed girls have joined in the revels, the hard work of all concerned yields its quota of laughs.'[5]

Crawford, who stayed in the play for more than a year before handing over to David Jason, said during its run, 'All your career as an actor you dream of having the things written up outside the theatre which are there about me – but now that they're there it's in a way the worst thing that could happen to me. I dread walking past them. Because every person who comes in thinks "this geezer's gonna make me laugh because it says here he recalls Harold Lloyd, he's a comic genius and he's a continual delight". It's all too fantastic. It really makes you want to work your arse off.'[6]

This was his first major starring role in the West End and he could be pleased with the rave notices, but there was one tinge of disappointment. 'What saddened me about the reviews,' said Crawford[7], 'wasn't so much that they had a go at the play, but they didn't recognise all the work done for me by the rest of the

73

team. Anthony Valentine does a thankless task and works like mad for me, and it all went unrecognised by the critics.'

Despite the critics, No Sex, Please was soon playing to capacity audiences, including a coach party from the Battersea pub whose darts team had kept Crawford busy during his period of unemployment. They brought with them a bag of tomatoes and a giant panda; they had nicknamed Crawford 'Panda' because of all the bruises his body had accumulated.

Crawford was giving his all to the show. Each day he would arrive at the theatre at two or three in the afternoon, long before the 7.30pm performance. He walked around the stage, perfecting his stunts, or just slept in his dressing-room or paced the empty corridors. The physical demands of the play meant that he had to drink three pints of water off stage during each performance to make up for what he was losing on stage.

When he was asked to star in a film version of No Sex, Please, Crawford turned down the offer. 'I don't like the way they want to make the film,' he said at the time[8]. 'The producers are trying to make all the characters funny, not just the one I played. I don't want to seem big-headed but I frankly don't think it will work. So I thought it better to withdraw before we got into production and arguments.' He was also concerned that his reputation might be tarnished by the way his physical comedy was edited. 'I'm very disappointed not to be doing the film,' Crawford added, 'but I would rather that people remember enjoying my performance in the play than say that I didn't quite pull it off in the film.' The role of Runnicles in the film was played by TV comedian Ronnie Corbett.

One film part that Crawford did accept was that of the White Rabbit in Alice's Adventures In Wonderland, which he made by day at Pinewood Studios during the stage run of No Sex, Please. Josef Shaftel, who had intended to cast him as Timothy Evans in The Christie Murders, before the plans fell through, was the producer of this live-action musical version of Lewis Carroll's story, best known on the screen as a Walt Disney cartoon[9].

The film was disappointing, despite a line-up of stars that included Peter Sellers, Sir Robert Helpmann, Dudley Moore, Sir Ralph Richardson, Dame Flora Robson, Michael Jayston, Spike Milligan, Sir Michael Hordern, Ray Brooks and Roy Kinnear.

Fiona Fullerton, then only fifteen and in her third feature film, played Alice. Director William Sterling had spotted a Sunday magazine photograph of her taken by Lord Snowdon, arranged to meet her and shortlisted her with two other girls to meet Shaftel; after a couple of screen tests in full costume, she was offered the role.

Many of the stars were hidden or semi-hidden behind masks, but their costumes were impressive and the sets were stunning, based on the original Tenniel drawings. William Sterling, born in Australia, with television experience there and in Canada and Britain, also wrote the screenplay. It was his feature film début, and he assigned two Oscar-winners, composer John Barry and lyricist Don Black, to write the musical score. Distinguished cinematographer Geoffrey Unsworth was the lighting cameraman.

Sterling said at the time, 'In my opinion, no one has yet caught the real spirit of *Alice* on the screen. No other medium can do Lewis Carroll's stories full justice. They cry out for the magic of the modern movies. Our aim is to make *Alice* a Victorian coloured picture book come to life on the screen, with all its charm, fun, fantasy and sense of magical wonder and adventure.'[10]

Unfortunately, despite such an illustrious cast and behind-the-scenes team, Sterling's picture lacked the 'magical wonder and adventure' for which he was looking.

Publicity for the film started badly when the American distributors flew 140 journalists and potential exhibitors to Britain. The aim was to give the writers the advance information they always sought and to gain interest from cinemas. The press were unhappy with the limited space on the plane and accommodation at their hotel, near Heathrow airport but a fifteen-dollar taxi ride from the centre of London. Those writers who travelled from Los Angeles had a twenty-four-hour journey and were called to a Peter Sellers press conference less than three hours after they arrived in Britain. Everyone was shown sequences and 'rushes' from the filming that had already taken place, but they were roughly put together and hardly impressive. This screening came at about midnight, after a traditional Elizabethan dinner and free drinks, with an 8.30am departure due the following day. 'Never, ever, should they unveil a picture in this state to anybody,' wrote Arthur Knight in *The Hollywood Reporter*[11].

American and British reviewers gave the film a thumbs-down

when it was released at the end of 1972. 'Superior stylistic settings and often terrific process effects are largely wasted by the limp, lifeless pacing of adapter-director William Sterling,' wrote *Variety*[12]. 'Having decided to make it a musical,' wrote Alexander Stuart in *Films and Filming*[13], 'William Sterling should have had his team work on the songs until they were really worth including – until they added something to the tale.'

Marjorie Bilbow, in *CinemaTV Today*, described the production as 'very plodding and unimaginative'[14], and Clyde Jeavons wrote in the British Film Institute's *Monthly Film Bulletin*, 'Apart from accommodating a number of half-hearted and totally unmemorable songs and dance routines, William Sterling has taken few liberties with the original narrative, but at the same time he has divested it of both its charm and its potential for cinematic comic invention. Visually the film is closer to a Babycham commercial than a Tenniel illustration.'[15]

By the time *Alice's Adventures In Wonderland* was released, Crawford and wife Gabrielle had split up, but they kept their parting quiet from the press for eighteen months. While making the film, Crawford had been getting up at 4.30am each day, going to the studios, performing on stage in *No Sex, Please – We're British*, then going to bed after 11pm.

He was taking large quantities of vitamin pills to keep his strength up – with the unexpected side-effect of giving him hairs on his chest – and he was socializing again, accepting invitations in the belief that it was necessary to circulate after his period in the wilderness. Soon the strain was showing and his home life was going wrong.

Crawford recalled, 'I was thinking: "This is the only work you've done for a long time. Don't spoil your chance." It was a wide-awake nightmare! All I could do was shout at Gabrielle and frighten her. We seemed to have gone past talking to each other and one day Gabrielle took the children off to her parents and just didn't come back.'[16]

Gabrielle felt that he was cutting her, Emma and Lucy out of his life. He had found a mews flat in Fulham, convenient for his work, but he often returned to his family only at weekends. 'I never left him,' she said[17]. 'He was living elsewhere. No man can have two homes, and the children were getting old enough to ask where their father was.' Eventually she confronted him. 'It came to the stage when I was married to Michael but seeing him once a week,' said Gabrielle[18]. 'In the end, I told him I wanted more of a family life. And he told me that if that was the case I would have to find somebody else.' Crawford stormed out and did not return for two weeks, and then only to pick up his mail.

Nine months after splitting up with Crawford, Gabrielle began a relationship with Chelsea footballer Tommy Baldwin, who had also parted from his wife. Only a few weeks after the Crawfords' split had made newspaper headlines, Gabrielle was named as 'the other woman' in a divorce action being brought by Baldwin's wife. When the case came to court, Pauline Baldwin was granted a decree nisi because of her husband's admitted adultery, but the judge found no evidence proved against Gabrielle. Baldwin and both women agreed in court not to talk to newspapers about the case.

The Crawfords' divorce followed in October 1975. Gabrielle was granted a decree nisi in a five-minute hearing at the Divorce Court in London, on the grounds that the couple had been apart for more than two years. They were given joint custody of Emma and Lucy, with Gabrielle having care and control. Crawford was not at the hearing; he was at the London Palladium, rehearsing for a Royal Variety Performance. As she left court, journalists asked Gabrielle how she felt. 'I can't say I'm exactly happy,' she replied[19]. 'Divorce is not an achievement, is it?'

Gabrielle went to stay with her parents in the Kent countryside for a few days after the hearing, collected her thoughts and decided to carve out a life for herself and her children. 'You either sink or swim,' she said[20], 'and I'd decided I was going to swim.'

She had already opened her own secondhand clothes shop, The Frock Exchange, in rented premises in Fulham Road, near Chelsea Football Club's ground. Now she began to treat the shop more as a business than a hobby, and expanded its services by offering home collection to rich women who would not be seen dead in a secondhand shop. 'In the beginning things were a struggle and I was a bit lonely,' said Gabrielle[21]. 'There was no real reason for it. The Frock Exchange had always been my baby. It was not something I'd ever discuss with Michael, because it didn't interest him.'

Soon Gabrielle opened another shop, Sign of the Times, selling cast-off clothes donated by stars such as Elton John, Clint

Eastwood and John Conteh, with the proceeds going to spina bifida sufferers. Her business partners were Tommy Baldwin, Chelsea footballer Charlie Cooke and Cathy McGowan, presenter of the Sixties TV pop show *Ready, Steady, Go!*

Gabrielle's relationship with Baldwin blossomed and they had two children together, Sam and Harry, but later the couple parted and she brought up the two boys.

Crawford was linked with several women after the break-up of his marriage. They included the pop singer Lyn Paul, best known as a former member of the New Seekers, dancer Jane Summerhayes, who appeared on the London stage in *A Chorus Line*, his secretary Jo-Anne Robinson, another dancer, who was in the musical *Billy* with him, and dancer Jane Watts, who appeared in *Barnum*. But he was to find no lasting romance again and, as the years went by, it became clear that he had not lost his love for Gabrielle. After the bitterness had gone, they forged a new friendship, but the flames of romance were not rekindled.

Chapter 11

SOME MOTHERS

As Crawford contended with heartbreak in his private life, his career soared to greater heights. He had done no regular television work since appearing as Byron in the mid-Sixties, but a BBC producer who saw him on stage in *No Sex, Please – We're British* realized that he was perfect for the lead role in a script submitted to him by a new TV comedy writer, Raymond Allen. The accident-prone Frank Spencer was just a step away from Runnicles, the witless bank clerk. Producer Michael Mills saw the opportunity to team up a new writer with an actor new to television comedy.

Allen lived on the Isle of Wight and had submitted dozens of scripts to the BBC and ITV, all of them turned down. 'I started writing scripts when I was fifteen,' he said[1], 'and I always wanted to be a serious writer. At the age of thirty, with about forty serious scripts rejected, I turned to comedy in sheer desperation. I broke in with sketches for Dave Allen and Frankie Howerd. Then I thought I would try writing a thirty-minute comedy play, which I sent to ITV and asked for their comments. They sent it back and tore it apart.

'In the meantime, I had written a second comedy script. I was a bit depressed about it and nearly didn't sent it off. It was about a young honeymoon couple, Frank and Betty Spencer. After eighteen years I was feeling everything was against me. When I wrote it in 1971 there was a postal strike, so I took it up to the BBC personally. I heard later from Michael Mills, at that time head of comedy, who said he liked the script and asked if I could do a series.'

Allen had never earned more than ten pounds a week, taking part-time jobs during the day so that he could write in the evenings. At the time he wrote *Some Mothers Do 'Ave 'Em* he was working as a cleaner in a cinema on the Isle of Wight. When he first had the idea for the programme, Frank Spencer was not even the main character. '*The Liver Birds* had just started on television,' recalled Allen[2], 'and I remember reading a bit in the paper saying there were very few situation comedies written for women, with women in the lead roles. I thought I wanted to write a situation comedy with a woman in the lead. It was Betty Spencer, and Frank was the idiot husband who said very little, just following her around. When I started writing it, I found I had more sympathy with Frank, and he started saying more and more, and Betty merged into the background.'

The script that Allen submitted to the BBC was intended as a single play. In looking for a situation, Allen recalled reading that a script was more likely to be accepted if there were few characters and few scene changes, making it cheaper to produce. So he set the play in a hotel room, and Frank and Betty Spencer were the honeymoon couple who booked in. Allen wondered what comedy they could get up to in a hotel room, and he decided they could smash the place up, with everything falling apart around them. This was how the visual comedy of *Some Mothers Do 'Ave 'Em* was conceived, although this was not to be the opening episode of the series; Michael Mills felt the couple needed to be introduced in another story, which saw Frank go for a job as a door-to-door salesman – one of many jobs – and bungle the practice session in his own inimitable way.

Allen drew on some of his personal exploits when coming up with ideas for the accident-prone hero. While working at the cinema, for instance, he tried to repair a cistern and ended up flooding the place. His unsuccessful serious plays had drawn on the Harold Pinter trick of having two different conversations continuing at the same time, and they were often returned with the comment that he had copied the playwright. Now he was able to use this style in comedy, to great effect. 'Frank would be having a conversation with someone,' said Allen[3], 'and, halfway through, he would talk about something that had absolutely nothing to do with it.'

All seven scripts were finished by the autumn of 1971, but the series was then almost never made. Duncan Wood, who had taken over from Michael Mills as BBC television's head of comedy, asked Allen to see Crawford on stage in *No Sex, Please – We're British*. 'I didn't like the show,' said Allen[4], 'but I thought Michael was brilliant, and he was already doing some of the Frank Spencer mannerisms. We didn't meet that night, but we went to a restaurant together a few weeks later and he said he was interested in the scripts. Then I went to see him at his home in Wimbledon and, as we were talking, he gradually got into the Frank Spencer character. He was illustrating to me how he would play it, but I didn't catch on immediately. Then I realized he was putting himself into the part.

'Just afterwards, he said he had decided not to do it because of other work commitments, so the project came to a halt as a result of the difficulty in finding an actor to play the part; it wasn't really a gag script – it was made for an actor more than a comedian. In the autumn of 1972, Michael came back and said he wanted to do it, so we took it from there.'

Crawford had finished his stage run of *No Sex, Please – We're British*, as well as the film *Alice's Adventures In Wonderland*. Now he could concentrate on his first television situation comedy series. In developing the character of Frank Spencer from Raymond Allen's scripts, he partly based it on a young man with bicycle clips whom he had seen in Battersea. 'He was pushing a pram with nothing in it and wanted to cross the road,' he recalled[5]. 'There was no traffic for miles, but he looked right and left for about five minutes and then something did come along and he was there for ages.'

The observant actor borrowed Frank's facial expressions from his younger daughter, Lucy. 'She'll start off,' he said at the time[6], 'with an appealing look like this [his eyes open wide and his jaw drops] and you can see her thinking: "No, I did that yesterday. That won't work, so I'll try it another way." Then she'll pout her lips and look cross, and you can still see her thinking: "No, I'm getting nowhere with that." So then a look of total bewilderment will spread across her face and, in the end, she'll just look appealing again and I always give in.'

Crawford also gave Frank a funny voice and walk, as well as a black beret and Army raincoat, which became his trademarks. 'I bought the clothes in a secondhand clothes shop near Edgware Road Tube station,' he said[7]. 'They obviously thought I was doing terribly badly at that time and were very pleased at how well they had rigged me out ... until I put on the mac. "I don't think that quite sets it off to the best advantage, sir." "No, no, no, I need it for something special." "Yes, I'm sure you do!" They probably imagined me as the gentleman flasher in the park!'

Frank also gave Crawford the opportunity to dream up stunts that would put his previous daredevilry in the shade. For the first series he simply embellished some of the ideas in Raymond Allen's scripts, which underwent constant rewriting until Crawford, Allen and producer Michael Mills were happy with the results. In subsequent series, Crawford would come up with the ideas, then Allen would write the episodes.

The stunts gave *Some Mothers Do 'Ave 'Em* a visual comedy that has not been seen on television before or since. One of Crawford's influences was Buster Keaton. 'Buster's one of my heroes,' he said[8], 'and I've admired the way he and other old-timers used to do their own stunts. I've always wanted to be like him. I believe it's much better for an audience to know I'm risking my neck rather than someone who looks like me. I suppose I might be trying to prove something to myself. Really, I'm just a frustrated sportsman. I like to show people I've got guts, although I've been scared at times.'

Crawford was teamed with Michele Dotrice, as Frank's wife, Betty. 'Ooh, Betty!' became a catchphrase as the screen calamities built up. 'I've had a bit of trouble,' was another familiar Spencerism. Dotrice, who comes from a showbusiness family – her father is actor Roy – had been acting since childhood and soon became known as the long-suffering wife of television's most disaster-prone character.

The first series, which began in February 1973 – with title music whose beat spelled out *Some Mothers Do 'Ave 'Em* in Morse Code – was an immediate success, entering the Top 20 TV ratings chart within three weeks. Viewers latched on to, and sympathized with, a vulnerable character who was unable to keep a job – as a security guard he lost his dog and as a fireman he kept missing the fire engine – and roared with laughter as his world collapsed around him.

The programme in which he was seen chasing his fire engine before it sped off drew some criticism from the Berkshire and Reading Fire Service. One sequence, filmed in Maidenhead, showed Crawford, dressed up in a fireman's uniform, peddling furiously on a bike in an attempt to catch up with the engine. 'It made a mockery of the fire service,' said the local assistant fire chief[9], but most people took the scene in good humour, as it was intended.

Crawford had more to worry about while filming a stunt at Stonebridge Park, more than one hundred feet above London's North Circular Road. He had to be seen in Frank Spencer's latest job, as a window-cleaner's assistant, in a cradle on the side of an office building. 'I can't stand heights,' Frank protests as his boss – played by stunt arranger Derek Ware – tries to calm him down. After a bit of clowning around, Frank drops his bucket twenty floors and the two fall out of the cradle, with Ware holding on to it and Crawford below him, gripping his ankles, as they dangle perilously in mid-air. The scene was filmed, but the problems started when they realized that it would not be possible for them to be lowered to the ground, as planned. While Crawford and Ware were in the cradle, it stayed upright; once they were over the side, it started tilting. If the cradle had been lowered, it would eventually have turned over, throwing out rigger Andy Bowman, who was controlling the stunt from inside it.

'Our combined weights on the outside of the cradle pushed it into the side of the building and made it tip,' said Ware[10]. 'We both had harnesses on and wires going into the cradle, so we were perfectly safe. Also, you're too preoccupied to be nervous. The rigger was in the more precarious position. He threw a rope-ladder down to Michael so that he could take the weight off his legs and the strain off his back. My legs went dead and, although I had a walkie-talkie, I could hardly speak because my right arm was wedged into my windpipe. Luckily, Andy cottoned on to what I was trying to say and took the cradle to the top of the building, where we had to jump six feet on to the roof. The problem with the building was that they had made it suicide-proof, so there were no windows you could open on the front.

'We were about twenty minutes altogether from the point where we realized they couldn't get us down to the time when we stepped on to the roof. To his credit, or possibly his ignorance, Michael then immediately filmed the next scene, where he had to be seen on the underside of a fire engine's turntable ladder twenty feet up in the air, being lowered to the ground. He said afterwards that, if he hadn't done that, he would never again have stepped even on a carpet.'

Ware, widely regarded as Britain's top TV stunt artist and arranger, ran an agency called Havoc, which advised Crawford on his dangerous routines throughout the first two series of *Some Mothers Do 'Ave 'Em*. 'Michael was a great listener,' recalled Ware[11]. 'When I was talking to him, he had this habit of looking over my head and I wondered whether what I was saying was going in, but he was digesting it and seeing how he could turn it round to his way of doing things. The only thing that made my hair stand on end was when I would say: "Dive through that window there and, as you go through it, hit it with your fists clenched together, tuck your head down in between on your elbows, get through and, as you go through, go into a roll." He would go through it sideways, with one arm out, turning his head to the camera. I would say: "You're going to break your neck." Then I began to realize why, and he said to me: "If I go through as you say, viewers can't see my face and they'll think we're using a double. I don't want to do a forward roll because that's what a stuntman does. Frank Spencer would slide along on his stomach."

'Before the first episode of the series, I was in a pub, talking to two other actors in the programme. They were saying what a stupid series it was, how ridiculous the character was, and it wouldn't get beyond the first episode. They thought Michael was an ego maniac. I don't think he is; he wants to be an entertainer. There's no actor in the world who has done all his own stunts. They always have a stunt co-ordinator and, usually, a stuntman waiting in the wings to do the "pick-up" shots later on. Michael's idol was Buster Keaton, and he had at the time studied Keaton more than I had, and said that he had never used a double. In fact, I now know of three occasions when he did use a double.'

When the series began, it was an immediate hit with viewers. Critics generally agreed it was funny, but some admitted to feeling uneasy about laughing at Frank Spencer as his world collapsed around him. Shaun Usher wrote in the *Daily Mail*, 'Nice guys, according to the cynical American saying, finish last. And Michael Crawford, one of the Nice guys, is finding it unexpectedly hard to win. *Some Mothers Do 'Ave 'Em*, his first television series, is funny enough. But some critics, and a number of ordinary viewers who have spoken to me about the show, feel rather uneasy. The trouble is that Crawford plays a foredoomed loser, and a lot of people find him far too likeable; they think it a bit rotten to keep having the laugh on him.'[12]

Matthew Coady wrote in the *Daily Mirror* that the programme was 'undeniably funny' but added, 'If comedy of this kind is to work, the actor must create a figure that transcends reality. Your laughter can be unrestrained only if you believe that nobody is getting hurt. In this case, Michael Crawford roused feelings of sympathy which, for me, blunted the joke.'[13]

Towards the end of the series, any TV critics who had their doubts about it were eating their words. Peter Black, whose *Daily Mail* colleague Shaun Usher had voiced reservations, wrote, 'Raymond Allen's *Some Mothers Do 'Ave 'Em* is the best visual comedy I've ever seen on TV. The Frankie character is one of those who in any crisis acts swiftly, decisively and disastrously. His young wife helplessly stands by, undefeatedly loyal.

'As in last night's script about the visit to the hospital, the invention of comic catastrophes is faultlessly logical and inexorable. Michael Crawford's and Michele Dotrice's timing, and the disciplined precision of complicated visual jokes, are brilliant. Michael Mills' production, always avoiding the self-consciously funny, has caught something of the style – and I choose the comparison with due care – of Laurel and Hardy.'[14]

Although Crawford had intended to do only one series of *Some Mothers Do 'Ave 'Em*, for fear of becoming typecast, the impact of Frank Spencer persuaded him to make another six episodes, which were broadcast at the end of 1973. 'It came as a bit of a shock,' recalled scriptwriter Raymond Allen[15]. 'I didn't realize there was going to be a second series. The second one was much more difficult because I had to come up with a script every couple of weeks, and there was so much crammed into each one. We would discuss themes, then I would go away and write them. There were also some running themes. Michael suggested Betty could have a baby, so we scattered bits of that story throughout the series.'

The stunts became more daring and, in one episode, Crawford found himself literally playing with fire, when what looked like fireworks were attached to the back of his jacket and suddenly had to start exploding. 'They weren't normal fireworks,' said Gavin Birkett[16], who was assistant floor manager on the first two series. 'They were special theatrical pyrotechnics that were fired electrically, using a detonator and a battery pack. His jacket was flame-proofed and we gave him protective padding at the back, just in case.'

That episode is a good example of another of the programme's secrets of success, packing so many different elements into half-an-hour. It begins with scenes of Frank Spencer in his latest, short-lived job as the skipper of a pleasure boat. The sight of the boat grounded on a mud bank and him holding a rope, looking for a tow, is followed by a 'Man Wanted' notice going up back at base. Walking home, he goes through one large garden gate, only to see the other one fall down.

In the house, wife Betty is phoning Dr Smedley to arrange an appointment for confirmation of her pregnancy, anxious not to tell Frank until she is sure, because of the shock it might cause him. She leaves, he believing she is going to the dentist. Dr Smedley confirms that Betty is pregnant and she returns home, where Frank is doing 'another little job' on a broken peddle-bin. Needless to say, the top subsequently shoots off. Betty gradually breaks the news to him and helps Frank to the sofa, where he asks, 'And can he tell? Just by looking at your teeth?'

Soon thrilling to the idea of becoming a father, Frank goes to Dr Smedley's maternity clinic to ask for advice, such as how to deliver the baby if it is born 'immaturely'. Told not to give Betty any sudden shocks, Frank sets off for another job interview, as an entertainer at a holiday camp. Waiting for him are the entertainments manager, played by veteran British character actor Sydney Tafler, and another stand-up act, in the guise of Christopher Timothy, who later became known as a star of *All Creatures Great and Small*. Timothy remarks, 'I see you've brought your costume.' Frank replies, 'I beg your pardon?' 'The funny beret and the Humphrey Bogart raincoat.' 'I always wear this,' Frank says, indignantly.

Then it is time for Frank to give a sample of his act, which is built around a ventriloquist's dummy called Marvin the Monkey.

Unfortunately the dummy has literally lost his head, after Frank backed the car over it, and it is being fixed. The replacement looks more like Popeye. Frank shows himself to be the only ventriloquist to move his lips but not his teeth. The entertainments manager wants to hear Frank sing and gears up for a rip-roaring session, at which the hapless hero launches into 'Early One Morning' – echoes of the audition Crawford did as a child for Benjamin Britten's production of *The Turn of the Screw*.

Timothy demonstrates the type of singing they are looking for and Frank latches on. His song is still 'Early One Morning', but it is more upbeat. Then comes the crowning glory of Frank's act, as he peels off his raincoat to reveal a smart suit underneath. Suddenly, his 'Vesuvius' erupts and there is smoke everywhere. Timothy and Tafler then spray foam at the fuming Frank, and it soon covers the entire stage. Frank is almost drowned in it, then pops up his head and says, 'Did I get the job?' That was one of the ad-libs to which the production crew gradually became used.

'Michael was very good at ad-libbing,' recalled Gavin Birkett[17]. 'He was very bright and quick off the mark. Sometimes there would be an extra pause that wasn't scripted, but which he felt was right at the time. That was quite difficult for the production team to follow. We wondered whether he had forgotten his lines but soon learned to let it go, rather than stop the recording. That was how he built something extra into the programme.'

One of the most dangerous stunts Crawford did in the new series was to hang on to the back of a car as it dangled over sea and rocks two hundred feet below. The only safety measures were two wires attached to him. This scene came towards the end of an episode in which Frank had already caused havoc in the local library, succeeded in unintentionally dismantling his neighbour's chicken house and attended an interview for a job selling farming products. Frank was successful in getting the job and was given a company car, an old Morris Minor, omitting to say that he was still learning to drive and wife Betty would always have to accompany him.

Then Frank and Betty are seen driving in the car at a clifftop beauty spot, where they get out and have a picnic. It starts raining and they rush for the car, where they have an afternoon sleep. When they wake up, everyone else has disappeared. They decide to go, too, but Frank has problems manoeuvring the car, whose tyres keep losing their grip. Suddenly the back of the Morris Minor is hanging over the cliff edge. Frank and Betty manage to get out and on to the bonnet, then he has the bright idea of removing a bag of manure from the boot. He clambers over the top of the car, with Betty holding his feet, only to end up with two shoes in her hands. Frank, meanwhile, is hanging from the back bumper. Soon he switches his grip to the exhaust pipe, which starts coming away. In the nick of time, a team of rugby players, passing in a coach, stop and pull the car – and Frank – to safety.

The scene was filmed at Swanage, in Dorset, and was reminiscent of Buster Keaton hanging over a waterfall in the 1923 silent classic *Our Hospitality*. Although Crawford had two safety wires attached to him, he succeeded in holding on to the car during all the filming. If he had let go, he would have fallen about thirty feet on to a narrow ledge, where boxes had been placed to break his fall.

'It was extremely dangerous because there would then have been another, hundred-foot drop off that cliff,' said stunt arranger Stuart Fell[18]. 'Michael Mills insisted that we had two safety wires on Michael, whereas stuntmen would normally work with just one. We ran them up his sleeve. He and Michele Dotrice were also on the top of the car at one point, and Michele was incredibly brave considering her fear of heights. She was fastened to a nylon tape, which we stuck to the vehicle; we filmed her close up and, wherever possible, I would hang on to her leg. Michael was also fastened on all the time.'

To make the car secure, railway sleepers were built into the cliff edge and joints were welded on to the bottom of the vehicle, acting as hinges. A long pole was fitted to the front of it to control the swaying. Michael Mills directed some of the filming through binoculars from a yacht out at sea. 'The coastguard was constantly getting calls from ships concerned about this car over a cliff edge and someone dangling from it,' recalled Stuart Fell[19]. 'It's very exhausting hanging on by your arms, and Michael had a strength in his upper arms that was out of proportion to the rest of his body. He also had a lot of bottle.'

Stunts brought *Some Mothers Do 'Ave 'Em* plenty of laughs, but the programme was certainly not reliant on them. The scripts were of a very high standard and, even when the obvious was about to happen, Raymond Allen's writing and the performances of Crawford and Michele Dotrice – especially their comic timing – provided moments of dialogue to treasure.

James Cossins, who had worked with Crawford on stage in *The Anniversary* and in the film *How I Won the War*, remembered his guest appearance in *Some Mothers Do 'Ave 'Em* as a pompous man running a public relations weekend course that Frank attended. A long scene at the blackboard with an awkward customer among his ranks worried the actor. 'Michael could make me laugh very easily,' said Cossins[20]. 'There were "takes" that were far longer than we had rehearsed, because of the pauses and looks he added. I prayed that we wouldn't crack up in laughter. The week before, they had recorded an episode with Fulton Mackay as an RAF psychiatrist interviewing Michael. The scene was done in front of a studio audience and Fulton had broken up completely. For him to break up was unheard of.'

Cossins also filmed a sequence with Crawford on Wimbledon Common, shown behind the end titles, in which Frank Spencer was running away from the grounds where the course was being held, with the organizer chasing him. 'That same day,' recalled Cossins[21], 'he filmed part of a terrifying scene on rollerskates where he went underneath a lorry. We all held our breath.'

For Crawford, it was all in a day's work, and split-second timing was the key. After being seen whizzing out of the doors of a rink, he had to skate at speed along a footpath of the common, round a spiral pedestrian walkway, on to a road, grab the back of a passing bus, let go, cut across a main road between cars coming in both directions, go across another road – between the wheels of a moving articulated lorry – and end up in a babywear shop, somersaulting into a cot.

The filming was done in Wimbledon and near London's North Circular Road, with Marc Boyle and Val Musetti arranging the stunts. They drove the cars travelling in opposite directions as Crawford rollerskated out of a side road. 'We worked out a rough stopping position, whether Michael was there or not,' said Boyle[22]. 'We had to work to him because he didn't have any brakes and had to put his faith in us. I was very worried about how he would cope because of the different surfaces of the road. If he'd hit a few bumps in the road, it could have ended up wiping his face out, but he did very, very well.' The lorry driver was real, not a stuntman, because it was thought no one else would have the expertise to drive a long, heavy vehicle at a specific speed. The stunt was practised in slow motion, before the cameras rolled and captured Crawford zooming between the lorry's wheels as it moved at fifteen miles per hour.

That scene ended an episode that also saw Frank and Betty taking two children to the zoo. He finished up in the chimpanzees' cage, hanging from the bars, while trying to retrieve his beret, stolen by one of the animals. Then one of the chimps, Judy, tried to pull Frank's trousers off. Unseen by viewers was another incident during the filming at Twycross Zoo, in Leicestershire, when Crawford and Michele Dotrice were outside the cage. 'Judy took a fancy to me and got very jealous of Michele,' he recalled[23]. Then he offered sweets to Judy and two other chimps. 'They nearly pulled me through the bars,' he said. 'It was the most frightening experience I've had in the series.'

The only injury Crawford sustained in making the second series was when he stubbed his finger while inside a wardrobe that tumbled down a flight of stairs in an episode about Frank attending an RAF reunion. It was an especially frightening stunt to do because he was in the dark and had very little control over what was happening. That was the story that finished with psychiatrist Fulton Mackay being driven almost insane – and to unscripted laughs during the first 'take'.

This series ended with the birth of Frank and Betty's baby daughter, Jessica. The story was based on the real-life birth of Crawford's younger daughter, Lucy, and had him on the hospital delivery table at one point, after fainting.

After a lucky thirteen episodes, Crawford decided that Frank Spencer should bow out. There was talk of a film based on the character, but that never happened, perhaps wisely in view of the disappointing transformation of many TV comedies to the big screen. As a television character, Frank had made his mark. After the episode with the rollerskating daredevilry, Mary Malone wrote in the *Daily Mirror*:

It isn't what Frank does that makes you laugh. It is what he fails to do. He is that rare thing, a chap who's made a hit by being passive.

Michael Crawford, who plays him, has the limp stance, the slack jaw, the boiled-eye stare off to perfection.

He is the perfect recipient of the custard pie. And the production team is in there working furiously to make sure the pies hit the target at a speed calculated to take your mind off the script, characters and relationships.

You can't say when yet another accident happens, 'Poor Frank!' We know by now that whatever he touches will break, fall, or explode.

He's just there, like weather. Every week, same old thing. Disaster rains down.

Last night started out with spilt acid and built up to a pellmell slide down stairs, across motorways, into a baby shop, on out-of-control roller-skates.

Marvellous, you say. Great. Now just how did they get the skates to do that? And how did they keep Frank upright on them?

The emphasis is all wrong. We should be laughing at Frank, not the mechanics that keep the comedy moving.

But, finally, I think I've got it – the secret of his success.

What's funny about Frank Spencer is that he's a fella.

For the script is written for Hilda Ogden, of *Coronation Street*.[24]

When *TV Times* readers voted Crawford 1973's Funniest Man on TV in the magazine's Top 10 Awards, it confirmed the phenomenal success that *Some Mothers Do 'Ave 'Em* had become in a short time. Barrister and writer Nemone Lethbridge, not a fan herself, wrote in *TV Times*, 'I cannot laugh at this massive dose of humiliation and embarrassment. Those who do love Frank (and they are legion) love him just because he is humiliated and embarrassed: they love him because he is vulnerable.'[25] She added, 'It takes the skill and discipline of the straight actor to create the funny man. To behave with such lack of physical balance takes the toughness and control of an athlete or ballet dancer. Just watch Michael Crawford walking into a wall or, as usual, falling about ... he has all the timing of the professional clown. One is reminded of the mime of Marcel Marceau .... You either love or hate the custard-pie routine, adore or detest the Marx Brothers. In fact, Michael

Crawford takes the mechanical joke a stage further than any one before him: before the custard pie hits him he has already fallen.'

Crawford always insisted that he and Frank Spencer were two completely different people, but it was sometimes difficult to escape the comparisons. As the second series of *Some Mothers Do 'Ave 'Em* was about to begin, he drove to Birmingham to appear as a guest celebrity in the TV show *What's My Line?*

On the way home afterwards, the engine of his car started boiling over and he was stranded on a motorway junction in a thunderstorm. 'So I climbed into the back seat,' he recalled[26], 'stripped off the suit I was wearing and put on my pyjamas, thinking I could dry myself afterwards with the spare pair. I was out and under the bonnet when I got stopped by this policeman. Said I was distracting other motorists. Couldn't see it myself.'

Another mishap, this time from his younger days, might have found its way into *Some Mothers Do 'Ave 'Em*. In a launderette, he realized he had left some clothes out of the load, so he opened the door to add them. Water, foam and clothes gushed out of the machine on to the floor. Crawford scooped up the suds in his hands and put them back in the machine – through the open door. When he suggested using this story in the programme, the producer told him it was too silly and far-fetched, and viewers would never believe it!

One result of Crawford's new success was to satisfy his grandmother, Edith Pike, who had always wanted him to be a TV star. She longed for him to be in *Coronation Street*, and even wrote to Granada TV, trying to get him a role in it. He fell about laughing when his agent phoned him with this news. Later, Crawford arranged for her to meet one of her *Street* favourites, Margot Bryant, who played Minnie Caldwell.

Another effect of Frank Spencer's success was the fan-mail Crawford received from parents of handicapped children. 'One of them,' he recalled[27], 'had a son so paralysed that the boy couldn't even laugh. But they told me that "during your show we saw a flicker of response in his eyes for the very first time".'

Just before Christmas 1973, he was invited to visit hospitals and old people's homes in Edinburgh to present gifts and give a bit of festive cheer. While at the city's Royal Hospital, he took a detour to the maternity ward, where he caused one woman to laugh so much that she had to be whisked away quickly for a premature birth. Another woman who had already had her baby was in such fits of laughter that she split her stitches.

Frank Spencer had endeared himself to so many people that Crawford's wish to leave the character behind was tempered by the pleasure it had clearly brought. It was five years before he made another series, but in 1974 and 1975 he recorded Christmas specials.

The first one, running fifty-five minutes, attracted twenty-four million viewers. This time he was putting his heart into playing an angel in a Nativity play at the local church. Perhaps influenced by the parachuting entrance he had by then made in the stage musical *Billy*, Crawford appeared from the heavens, lowered by a wire and dressed angelically, complete with wings – and beret.

He was intended to come down at the wrong moment, disappear, do the same again, then go shooting through the roof when the mechanics of the wire go wrong. In reality, the mechanics went wrong when he first appeared and shot him into the air, out of sight. Everyone in the studio burst into hysterical laughter. 'The camera crew were shaking with laughter,' recalled Gavin Birkett[28]. 'We had to stop recording. It was five or ten minutes before they and the studio audience could control themselves. In the end, we decided to use that unscripted version.'

In the story, Frank had to be seen shooting through the roof of the church moments later and holding on to a cross, before being rescued by a helicopter. For the exterior filming, stunt arranger Stuart Fell found a church at Runham, in Norfolk, which had lost its roof. 'We added our own,' he said[29], 'which meant putting rubber tiles on. It was an extremely windy day, and we had problems keeping them down. Marc Boyle was brought in to help me and, when everything was ready, he and I stood Michael on a wooden tray, lifted it up and threw him through the roof.'

The cross was constructed specially and came off the church roof with Crawford as he was winched away by a Wessex helicopter. 'The idea was that he would be taken up a couple of hundred feet,' said Gavin Birkett[30]. 'It was for the end-title sequence, and Michael Mills liked to have too much film rather than not enough, so the camera was still turning over when Michael got to just under a thousand feet!'

The following Christmas, more than twenty-five million viewers watched a forty-five-minute special in which Frank is sacked from his seasonal job as a pixie in a grotto, before winning a Do It Yourself Man of the Year award, for which Betty has entered him. When a television crew turns up for a tour of his house and DIY achievements, everything falls apart as he touches it. The programme was beaten in the TV ratings only by the ever-popular *Morecambe and Wise Christmas Show*, which attracted twenty-eight million viewers, the highest figure for any programme in eight years. Apart from repeats, Frank Spencer would not be seen again until 1978.

Chapter 12

BILLY

The musical *Billy* gave Crawford a chance to consolidate his previous stage success, with *No Sex, Please – We're British*. This production was based on the famous Keith Waterhouse novel *Billy Liar*, about an undertaker's assistant who escapes the dull routine of everyday life by entering a world of fantasy. The Fifties book had already been turned into a stage play by the author and Willis Hall in 1960. Both later adapted it into a film, starring Tom Courtenay and Julie Christie, and a television series. Dick Clement and Ian La Frenais, who had written one of Crawford's films, *The Jokers*, now turned it into a musical, with a score by John Barry and lyrics by Don Black, who had both written the music for the film *Alice's Adventures in Wonderland*. Barry had also composed the music for *The Knack*, and raised the idea for *Billy* with producer Peter Witt over lunch a couple of years before it materialized.

This was the first London West End musical for both Crawford and director Patrick Garland, whose production of *Brief Lives* was a TV and theatre success, starring Roy Dotrice. 'The problem with big musicals,' said Garland[1], 'is that English directors haven't much experience with them. We have a grasp of classical theatre, but different nations have different talents, and the musical is not an indigenous art form. I made it a condition that I'd only do it with an American choreographer, and my assistant is American, too.'

The choreographer was Onna White, who had worked on the first musical version of a Charles Dickens book, *Oliver!*, the 1968 British film starring Ron Moody and Oliver Reed – for which she won a special Oscar – and had staged *Half a Sixpence* in New York, featuring Tommy Steele. White was born in Canada but had lived most of her life in America. The new musical was to open at the Palace Theatre, Manchester, for three weeks, before moving to the Theatre Royal, Drury Lane, in London's West End. Because the sets were completely different, the Theatre Royal having a much taller stage, White had to restage the movements during the two-week break. She had problems getting a work permit, which halved her time putting Crawford through his steps. She made him take tap classes to loosen his ankles and gave him daily exercises to do under her assistant's instruction. 'But I needn't have worried,' she said[2]. 'Michael is really exceptional. He has this lovely pixie body and whips off complicated tap routines in the Astaire and Gene Kelly styles – amazing. He's so good that I've ended up basing all my choreography around him.'

In the show, Crawford did a song-and-dance impersonation of Fred Astaire up a lighted stairway. He felt that his experience in the film *Hello, Dolly!* had given him the confidence to do *Billy*, and he remained grateful to Gene Kelly, who had helped him so much during the picture's making. Before rehearsals started, he got himself in trim by running every day, knowing that he would have to be ultra-fit for each night's three-hour performance, appearing on stage for almost every minute of it.

Billy also featured Diana Quick and Elaine Paige – who had performed in the musicals *Hair, Jesus Christ Superstar* and *Grease*, and would later star in Andrew Lloyd Webber's *Evita* and *Cats* – with Bryan Pringle and Avis Bunnage as Billy's parents. Peter Bowles played the lad's boss, Mr Shadrack, in the Manchester production, but Christopher Hancock took over when the show moved to London.

The Manchester première in March 1974 had to be cancelled when Crawford went down with laryngitis. When *Billy* finally opened, it was an immediate hit, the lavish production opening spectacularly with Crawford descending forty feet on to the stage by parachute, with the help of a harness. 'I have a little prayer I say three times before I come down,' he said at the time[3]. 'When I'm coming down in that parachute, I'm feeling pretty nervous, but it's wonderful the way I can feel the audience reacting warmly towards me.'

96

On one occasion Crawford was left hanging above the stage for ten minutes when there was a bomb scare and everyone left the theatre quickly, forgetting that the top-of-the-bill was at the top of the stage. On another night, he went on for his Fred Astaire routine, after one of three ultra-quick changes, with his flies open. The zip had become stuck, his musical cue came and he had no alternative but to go back on stage, in a routine that included some big kicks.

Worse was to come when the left-handed star broke his left hand while swinging on scaffolding. 'I forgot to wipe the sweat off my hands when I started swinging,' he said[4], 'and my hands were so slippery that I fell.' The demanding role meant Crawford had no understudy to begin with, so he carried on with a wrist cast, and Onna White changed the choreography to allow for this.

During the two-week break before *Billy* opened in London, White revised the whole show's choreography to make the most of designer Ralph Koltai's massive sets, which included staircases appearing and disappearing, scenes sliding off and on, high overhead platforms sliding forward for dancers, a back projection screen being lowered, and streams of coloured lights.

Peter Bowles left the show, as did his song, 'Shadrack and Duxbury'. Another number, 'That Wouldn't Be You', was replaced by 'Is This Where I Wake Up?', sung by Crawford, Diana Quick and the dancers, who included Suzanne Danielle and Jo-Anne Robinson, who subsequently became the star's secretary and girlfriend. The lyrics of 'That Wouldn't Be You' resurfaced four years later in a musical version of the Jack Rosenthal television play *Bar Mitzvah Boy*, although they were slightly revised, as indicated by the new title, 'You Wouldn't Be You'.

By the time *Billy* opened at the Theatre Royal, Drury Lane, Crawford had a standby, Billy Boyle, but he had other worries. Aware that *Some Mothers Do 'Ave 'Em* had a massive audience, ranging from children to grandparents, Crawford said[5], 'I then go and put myself before the public' as Billy Liar, whose first words as he comes on stage are along the lines of "Christ Almighty, bloody, blimey!" in a song. Well, a few of my sweet old ladies are going to have palpitations. It's all humour, it's all funny, but it's not the gentle humour of Frank.'

At the Theatre Royal, Crawford had a dressing-room, complete with velvet curtains and luxurious couch, that had once been used by Ginger Rogers, when she was starring in a London stage version of the hit Broadway musical *Mame*. On the wall, the new star mounted a photograph of Gene Kelly, who came to see him and told him how proud he was of his performance, and painted on the door were the words 'Ginger Crawford'.

Appearing at Drury Lane was a dream come true for Crawford, who had previously been there just once, in the audience watching Julie Andrews in *My Fair Lady*. He could not sleep for two days before *Billy's* first night, on 1 May 1974, and he was unable to eat during the day of the opening show, which was attended by Princess Margaret and the Queen Mother. He was still nursing his hand wound and was in pain for most of the evening, but his all-singing, all-dancing performance brought him a standing ovation and fifteen curtain-calls at the end of three magical hours. Then, with the curtain down, members of the cast started applauding Crawford's glittering performance. 'It was too much,' he said[6], 'and I broke down and cried.'

At a party after the show, he was the toast of the West End. Lauren Bacall, Bianca Jagger, Claire Bloom, Linda Thorson and Lionel Blair were among the stars who showered him with praise. Then Crawford went out for a welcome late-night meal, before staying up to read the reviews in the early editions of the next day's newspapers.

Apart from a few critics' reservations about the strength of the show's songs, the reviews saluted Crawford as the West End's newest star. Herbert Kretzmer wrote in the *Daily Express*, 'Whether making his entrance by parachute, dancing like Fred Astaire, or impersonating Elvis Presley in a loud, long rock number, Crawford rides triumphantly to stardom.'[7] In the *Daily Mail*, Jack Tinker wrote:

THERE IS no magic quite like being right there when a star is born. In this case, reborn. Michael Crawford's career, until now, has been a series of brilliant firework bursts which have never quite ignited into an enduring setpiece that sets the sky alight.

But last night Michael Crawford took his cue from Don Black's recurring lyric: 'Some of Us Belong to the Stars' and the glittery Drury Lane first-nighters shared his ascent among the galaxy to the ever-resounding echo.

Of course the show is designed to give him rocket-powered lift-off. It must be one of the few British musicals to make one feel chauvinistically inclined to announce one's origins.

As the musical of the film of the play of the book it has, to say the least, a distinguished pedigree. Keith Waterhouse's original novel, *Billy Liar*, was one of the minor masterpieces of the Sixties [*sic*]. It encapsulated all the preoccupations and fantasies of the provincial adolescent.

The play, which Waterhouse adapted with Willis Hall, had the distinct dramatic disadvantage of confining Billy's clamouring imagination to a drab, realistic setting.

But the musical is a vehicle to liberate all the pent-up frustrations of Billy's fantasia.

When Mother – the marvellous Avis Bunnage, resisting all temptation to caricature – calls him down to breakfast, Crawford descends from the flies in a parachute. He is in Billy's make-believe world of ambrosia the moment the curtain rises. A dream citadel where Billy escapes from his day-mare realities.

To be ruthlessly honest, the choreography of American-imported Onna White hardly soars to the possibilities of the book or indeed to Ralph Koltai's adaptable setting.

Koltai suggests everything appalling in modern urban life: The Wimpy-precinct existence which one realises with something like delayed shock is just as inescapable now as it was in the Fifties when Billy first sought refuge in his compulsive make believe.

Perhaps this is what makes Michael Crawford's triumph so appealing. To see him Fred Astaire-ing in white tie and tails down stairways which light at the touch of a toe, or pelvising his way through lurex-decked rock and roll routines, is to sit at the ringside of every trapped soul's private escape hatch.

Indeed the show is strangest at its saddest. And director Patrick Garland gives these tender moments (notably Lockwood West wistfully singing 'It Were All Green Hills') as much emphasis as the noisy production numbers.

In an evening which belongs to Michael Crawford, it would

be ungracious not to notice with gratitude Bryan Pringle's blaspheming father, Gay Soper's virginal fiancée, and Diana Quick's electrifying Liz.[8]

The magnitude of Crawford's performance was summed up by Sheridan Morley in *The Tatler*: 'In the end it is Mr Crawford's evening: he turns in the kind of all-singing all-dancing performance that legends are made of, and the kind that an English actor hasn't achieved since Buchanan[9] in the 30s.'[10] Elaine Paige remembered the energy he put into giving pleasure to the audience. 'If he tried to get a laugh and it wasn't successful, I could see him bristle,' she said[11]. 'He was quite temperamental because of his perfectionism, and he was always concerned that there was something he was not doing with the material; in other words, he blamed it on his delivery.'

Crawford's grandmother, Edith Pike, went to see the show three times. On the last occasion, she was given a seat in the Royal Box. Normally she would sit in the audience chattering to those around her about her grandson on stage, and miss some of the dialogue. This time she heard him use a rude word, and said out aloud, 'Oh, Michael, you should never say that.' Crawford recalled[12], 'I couldn't believe my ears. The whole cast broke up. They were creasing themselves. The show just came to a standstill, and the audience didn't know what was happening. All you could hear was her tut-tutting.'

Billy quickly broke box-office records at the Theatre Royal, playing to capacity audiences after its second week. In its first five weeks, the show took £132,000, plus ten per cent VAT.

After four months in the West End, Crawford was ordered by doctors to take a twelve-day rest to recover from a severe back strain, but he returned in time to appear in front of Prince Charles. A year later he collapsed from exhaustion but insisted in carrying on with eight shows a week. The theatre management urged him to take a holiday, but he refused, not wanting to disappoint the audiences who were still rushing to get seats at each performance.

He finally took the advice of doctors a month later, and he went on a two-week holiday to Jamaica. This came shortly after wife Gabrielle had been granted a decree nisi in a divorce court, while Crawford was rehearsing at the London Palladium for a Royal

Variety Performance, which included excerpts from *Billy*. Unfortunately most of what ITV screened came from the cast's rehearsals, not the actual performance, and television mogul Lew Grade sent the cast an apologetic telegram afterwards.[13]

In May 1976 Crawford left *Billy*, after two years in the show. His last performance was another sell-out, ending with scenes of adulation normally reserved for pop stars. Little more than twenty-four hours later, he was in hospital for an operation on damaged arteries in his legs, the price of making people laugh.

Roy Castle took over the starring role for the show's last nine weeks but was worried that some of the language would tarnish his reputation as a family entertainer. 'I wasn't too keen on two or three of the swear words,' he said[14], 'and I asked if I could leave them out. There was a newspaper reporter who made a meal out of it. It made my life a bit unbearable for a while and made it look as if I was attacking Michael, which I wasn't.'

Chapter 13

SAME TIME, DIFFERENT ACTRESS

Even before Crawford left the cast of *Billy*, it was announced that he would be starring in a London West End production of Bernard Slade's award-winning Broadway play *Same Time, Next Year*. It was still running in New York, where Ellen Burstyn had won a Tony award for her performance as the mistress whose married lover conducts their affair on a once-a-year, same-time-same-place basis. The play was a two-hander, which meant that it was carried from beginning to end by the two stars.

Crawford was paired with actress Frances Cuka, who had spent much of her career with the Royal Shakespeare Company and was returning to Britain after playing Mrs Lenin in its Broadway production of *Travesties*. She had also made her mark in the plum role of Jo in the original London and Broadway productions of *A Taste of Honey*, Shelagh Delaney's play about a working-class girl who reluctantly faces motherhood after an affair with a black sailor, and finally chooses a life without men. Written at the end of the Fifties, it was a play ahead of its time, tackling issues of illegitimacy and inter-racial relations with a feminist approach, and set Cuka off on a distinguished career.

After Crawford's three-month break, during which he got sunstroke and fell down in the garden, breaking two bones in his foot, he and Cuka started rehearsals. There would be a two-week run at the Theatre Royal, Norwich, before opening at the Prince of Wales Theatre on 23 September 1976. Crawford ensured that no one under fourteen would be allowed into the performances because of the strong language and much hopping in and out of bed – and he

102

banned his grandmother. He and Cuka had an agreement not to have garlic with their meals. 'We're on stage together the whole evening, playing very close,' he said[1]. 'It's instant love from eight o'clock onwards.'

In the show, set in a California motel, they had to age twenty-five years, which meant six complete changes of costume, hairstyle and make-up. At the beginning, Crawford's character, George, was given grey hair underneath a dark spray, which was slowly wiped away. This was preferred to the normal process of simply making the hair greyer, and the stars did not like the set of wigs that was originally intended to be used.

Same Time, Next Year was generally well received. Whether Crawford liked it or not, critics and audiences found it difficult to watch this new character without Frank Spencer and his other previous creations in the back of their minds. This was not a musical, and there were no deliberate clangers or daredevil stunts. The reviews reflected this difficulty of critics to come to terms with Crawford in a production so different from his biggest successes. As an actor, that was of course his aim.

Jack Tinker wrote in the *Daily Mail*, 'Not only do we grow to know the entire family environments of George and Doris (well, even names like that deserve romance) but we see the passing parade of America's social life over quarter of a century. But it is the immaculate artistry of Michael Crawford and Frances Cuka that makes us care. Mr Crawford proves that if he has not buried the Frank Spencer TV image, at least he is not here to praise it. The evening is the finest that commercial theatre has the right to expect.'[2]

John Barber of the *Daily Telegraph* observed that the therapeutic effect of the couple's five yearly meetings helped to save each of their marriages. 'What saves the play from its Broadway wisecracks and theatrical chicanery,' he added[3], 'is the truth of Frances Cuka's playing. In no way glamorous, a cuddly bundle of soft feminine humanity, she expresses Doris's sweetness as powerfully as her animal desires. As George, Michael Crawford's gangling, adolescent-grown-up charm is valuable, but he finds the comedy within his range and some emotional moments less comfortable. The direction of Eric Thompson is beyond praise.'

After that first night, Herbert Kretzmer wrote in the *Daily Express*:

MICHAEL CRAWFORD, after playing for years a succession of wistful or gormless youths, last night took on a role in which he is required to age a quarter of a century.

The roar of the crowd that greeted the final curtain seemed to confirm that Crawford, who has long nourished an ambition to bring this still-running Broadway hit to London, has chosen his moment well.

Same Time, Next Year is a lively, humorous account of a developing relationship, at first sexual but later broadening into a touching tenderness, of two people long married to others, who meet once every year in a California motel for what used to be called 'a dirty weekend'.

He is a green, insecure accountant from New Jersey on a once-a-year trip to the West Coast. She is a middle-American matron on her way to a Catholic retreat.

Between them they have seven children. Neither are promiscuous. Their annual tryst is their only departure from their marriage vows.

Over six acts, ranging from 1951 to 1976, we watch Crawford ringing in the changes from timid, guilt-ridden husband to an angry right-winger who votes for Barry Goldwater, finally to a mature widower, afraid of a lonely old age.

Similarly, we are drawn into the life changes of the woman, played with affecting insight by Frances Cuka.

Embracing the traumatic years of Vietnam, Kennedy, the Beatles and Watergate, *Same Time, Next Year*, by Bernard Slade, is a well-crafted comedy of social change and personal discovery that I predict will take root in the West End for long months to come.[4]

In January 1977, amid rumours of a personality clash with Crawford, Frances Cuka left the production, exercising a clause in her contract that allowed her to go after four months. At the time she did not publicly disclose why, saying only, 'I am leaving for reasons which I cannot say. There are other personalities involved and I do not want to hurt anybody. It is a lovely play and I am sorry to be leaving, but this is a very strenuous role, and what I am doing is perfectly normal. I do not want to go into detail about how I get on with Michael. No, I would not object to working with him again.'[5]

During the two years of the Broadway production, there had been frequent changes of cast, but backstage staff at the Prince of Wales Theatre talked of a growing gap in the working relationship between Crawford and Cuka, and the management eventually admitted there had been a 'personality conflict'. In an effort to force management to give a fuller public explanation, front-of-house staff threatened to strike and backstage staff to give in their notice. In the end, they agreed it was in everyone's interest to carry on working, and the show was not threatened.

For her last week, Cuka had been appearing with understudy Richard Franklin because Crawford had laryngitis. He said, 'Michael and Frances are two very strong and different personalities and they clashed.'[6] Cuka's understudy, Gloria Connell, who stood in opposite Crawford for a week, said, 'There were no public rows between the two, but it's true to say the atmosphere was very cool.'[7]

Eight months later, Cuka hinted briefly at her reasons for leaving the show. The play was meant for two stars, 'not a star and a satellite,' she said[8], adding, 'It was all very depressing, but I'm not hurt. You can be hurt only by someone for whom you care.'

At the time of her departure, theatre staff talked of Crawford's practice of giving 'notes' – verbal criticisms of each actor's performances. One of them said he was 'so fussy that he moaned about the smallest things – like the position of Miss Cuka's arms in a scene'[9]. Crawford explained, 'Throughout my acting career, I have always taken notes of myself from directors and from actors. That's how one learns a performance. And I firmly believe in giving notes to others to ensure that the standard set on the first night is maintained.'[10] Inevitably, if there were only two people in a stage play, the full weight of one actor's criticism would fall on the other.

Crawford immediately brought in as Cuka's replacement his *Some Mothers Do 'Ave 'Em* screen wife Michele Dotrice. She took over after a week's rehearsal, during which Cuka's understudy, Gloria Connell, played opposite Crawford. It was a case of Crawford bringing in someone with whom he knew he could work. In May 1977 he, too, left the show, having completed nine months in it. His replacement was comedy actor Derek Nimmo.

Talk of Crawford starring as Stan Laurel in a musical by Dick

Clement and Ian La Frenais, and as Charlie Chaplin in another musical, to be produced by Peter Witt and based on a Keith Waterhouse/Willis Hall story, came to nothing. After a year's break, Crawford was back at the BBC, making a final series of *Some Mothers Do 'Ave 'Em* and a play that would show his more serious side to a large audience, in the way that only television could do.

Chapter 14

GRANDMOTHERS, DISSIDENTS AND MOTHERS AGAIN

Turning down offers of work, Crawford took a rest after six exhausting years, during which he had bounced back from his film disappointments to become one of Britain's top television and stage stars. Looking for peace and solitude, he bought a cottage in a small Bedfordshire village and had a garage turned into a bungalow for his beloved grandmother. For a year, his new home came before work.

'I heard they were selling off some cottages on the Woburn Estate,' said Crawford shortly afterwards[1]. 'I thought that would be great. I'd have lions to guard me! When I got there, it turned out they were only leasing them, and I wanted the security of my own place. But there were some more in the same area. I looked at lots, and then I saw this fairytale cottage, like something out of *Alice In Wonderland*. I said "yes" there and then, and I absolutely adore it. Next door was an old brick garage, which I converted into a cottage for my Nan. She's ninety-three and totally blind. So I had it put all on one floor for her, so she wouldn't have any stairs to climb. I had always dreamed of living in the country. It was what I really wanted to do. No one can describe how wonderful the smell of the country is. It was a year of pure magic.'

During that year, Crawford also holidayed in Greece with his daughters Emma and Lucy. He had found little time for romance since his marriage ended. Former New Seekers singer Lyn Paul was linked with him briefly and, in a 'kiss and tell' interview, said, 'I think every time he took a girl out he compared her with his former wife, Gabrielle, and none of them came up to scratch.'[2] Another girlfriend was American actress Jane Summerhayes, one of the stars of the Broadway hit musical *A Chorus Line*, which came to London's West End in the baking summer of 1976. Soon he was spending most of his time rehearsing for *Same Time, Next Year* and she went back to America.

When Crawford returned to television, it was in a straight role very different from Frank Spencer. Before making another series of *Some Mothers Do 'Ave 'Em*, he starred in a BBC *Play for Today* double-bill, *Private View* and *Audience*, under the umbrella title *Sorry* .... Both plays were written by Czech dissident Václav Havel, who had been at the forefront in the battle against communism ever since Russian tanks rolled into Prague in 1968. He was one of the three original signatories to the human rights document Charter 77, after which he was arrested, and his writing and plays were banned in Czechoslovakia. For ten years, Havel had kept a small flame of dissent burning during Czechoslovakia's dark days under the thumb of Stalinism. His plays, performed in the West, ingeniously poked fun at the way in which the Party corrupted language – with echoes of Orwellian-speak – and maintained sinister undertones, in the chilling style of Kafka.

The central character in the *Play for Today* double-bill was Ferdinand Vanek, played by Crawford. He, too, was a writer and worked at a brewery – as Havel had done – keeping his thoughts to himself. The plays were about oppression, and producer Innes Lloyd and director Claude Whatham were anxious that a large audience should be made aware of the plight of Czech dissidents such as Havel. 'One of the reasons we did the play,' said Lloyd[3], 'was to make sure as many people as possible watched it; hence casting Michael in it. Therefore, we could spotlight that here was a writer standing up for his rights.'

It was Whatham who had the idea of casting Crawford, but the star best known to television audiences as a loveable idiot was not sure whether his presence would be beneficial to the plays. The director was determined to get his man. 'If I was coming home tired,' said Whatham[4], 'a play by a dissident Czech playwright would not be the first programme I would turn on. But Havel's plays, apart from being very penetrating, are very funny, and I wanted a cast who could play high comedy. The main character has to be played by somebody who has, to a great extent, worked in reaction. It seemed to me that somebody like Michael Crawford would be an absolute past master at giving a riveting performance by appearing to do almost nothing.

'His agent was sent a script and it was turned down. I rang his agent and said: "Do you think I could have his number so that I could persuade him?" The agent just gave it to me, which obviously meant he wanted him to do it and is unusual because they don't normally give out telephone numbers. I rang Michael and said I'd like to go over and persuade him, and drove to his cottage and talked at length about how I saw it and why I really wanted his sort of ability and personality. He thought about it over the weekend and accepted.

'It was rather touching that when I told him who the other members of the cast were – Ian Richardson, Zena Walker and Freddie Jones – he said: "Do they know who it is who's playing the character?" He was obviously very diffident about working with "classical" actors.'

In fact, the other members of the cast were wary of the actor whose leading lady, a classical actress, had walked out on him little more than a year earlier in the stage play *Same Time, Next Year*. 'There was a fair amount of nervousness on their part,' said Whatham[5]. 'At that time, Michael didn't have a very good reputation for being easy to work with.'

Freddie Jones recalled the reaction of other actors on hearing that he was appearing with Crawford. 'Beforehand, in an Acton pub near the rehearsal rooms, they asked what I was doing,' he recalled[6]. 'When I said I was working with Michael Crawford, they said he would be a monster, eat me for breakfast, have me on toast and upstage me totally. I began to get very worried. In the end, I thought: "I'm not in competition. This is a play." When we started rehearsing, I found him to be very friendly and lots of fun, like a younger brother or son.' Ian Richardson and Zena Walker also enjoyed working with him, and all three approached director Claude Whatham after the first week's rehearsals, saying they wanted to form a We Think Michael Crawford Is Marvellous Society.[7]

Each play was presented on a single set, as it would be in a theatre. In the first, *Private View*, Ferdinand is invited to see the redecorated flat and newly acquired possessions of two old friends,

Michael and Vera, played by Ian Richardson and Zena Walker. In between boasting about their materialistic possessions, the couple denigrate Ferdinand's lifestyle and marriage. Throughout, he is quiet and well mannered, but eventually he walks out on them, at which they make a big scene. They cannot face being left to their own, shallow life, which has no substance; conversely, Ferdinand gains inner strength from maintaining his stand against tyranny. The couple act as if nothing has happened when Ferdinand agrees to stay.

In the second play, *Audience*, Ferdinand is called in by the head maltster, played by Freddie Jones, who insists that he joins him for a drink and a chat. The drink becomes bottle after bottle of beer, which Ferdinand is reluctant to drink. It emerges that the head maltster has been asked to inform on his behaviour to the police. If Ferdinand will co-operate, perhaps there will be a better job for him at the brewery. On principle, Ferdinand refuses, and the head maltster realizes that this threatens him more than it does the writer.

'Freddie had to drink nineteen bottles of beer in the play,' said Claude Whatham[8]. 'You can't fake bottled beer; there's no way you can put in something that's innocuous and cap it, and part of the action was that Freddie had to take the cap off. Freddie resolutely refused to rehearse with water because he would have had to drink glass after glass and, being a bitter expert, he refused to drink bottled beer. There was a very strong rule that you don't have alcohol on working premises, only in the BBC Club. They were unlikely to provide an adequate quantity of unflat best bitter in the rehearsal rooms so by special dispensation we had two bottles of white wine per day, which, of course, were shared between him and Michael, who drinks very little. He was slightly perturbed by this but eventually found it very funny because rehearsals became very convivial. Both of them were very relaxed indeed.'

The biggest problem for Crawford and Jones was the script's 'spiral' technique, whereby the same dialogue is returned to constantly but in paraphrased form. 'For both of us, it was nightmarishly difficult,' recalled Jones[9]. 'For Michael, it was difficult because it was use of half-sentences, which were important. For me, it was the most teasing of all things, variations on a theme, slight changes. I would have to go off to the lavatory, come back and start the same scene with a variation. So when we came to record it, if there was a technical breakdown, we would rush to the corner of the set, grab the script and discover where we were.'

Claude Whatham arranged the recording to take account of this difficulty. He recalled, 'I told Freddie: "You are going to go wrong. When you do, we will keep the tape running and give you a cue line. When you are ready, go back as far as you want and we will pick it up from you." This happened three times during the recording; it was amazing that it wasn't more. The method of working was fine and you wouldn't have known there were any interruptions when you saw the programme.

'What surprised the crew was that Michael led the insistence on the part of the actors to record both plays again, having done them extremely well but feeling they could be done better. So we did them again, although we used the original as the "master" and intercut bits of the second recording. I had one camera on Michael all the time and recorded him separately, using fewer cameras on the rest of the action, because it was impossible from a rehearsal outside the TV studios to anticipate the reactions. Then, I edited it together afterwards.'[10]

Freddie Jones would never forget Crawford's enthusiasm and generosity of spirit during the recording, and afterwards. 'He was incredibly careful about my performance, as well as his own,' said Jones[11]. 'During the interruptions in recording, he would keep saying across the desk, "Keep the ball in the air, keep it going, keep it up. It's absolutely marvellous; it's going brilliantly." Having done the recording, I found myself in the dressing-room in tears. It had been so dramatic and difficult. I wondered if I had betrayed myself, just remembering the complexity. Then there was a knock on the door. I quickly got rid of the tears and there Michael was, saying wonderful, encouraging things. He said: "It's the best; it's wonderful."' Jones's modesty prevented him from speaking in public about the full extent of Crawford's praises. Claude Whatham revealed, 'Michael told him: "That was marvellous. You are the sort of actor I would like to be."'[12]

Jones recalled that people were questioning Crawford's motivation in doing the Havel plays, but he believed it was simple. 'All he wanted was to get into something serious,' said Jones[13]. 'The first time it was shown on television, I was watching my own performance and seeing how far it was from what I had conceived. It is always a series of disappointments with highlights in between. Then it was repeated late at night to salute Havel when he was sent to prison again. That time, I watched Michael's performance, which was stunning. I'm quite sure that it was a sort of catalyst for him, to prove that he could do something like that.'

Whatham's hunch in casting Crawford, who sported a neatly cut beard for the role, had been proved correct. 'I thought his performance was just masterly,' he said[14]. 'Without in any way undermining the importance of the character, he managed to be very, very funny, like in the business of getting rid of the beers that he didn't want. The same in the verbal playing, and without losing the underlying terror of the situation.'

The double-bill was also well received by TV critics in the more serious newspapers and magazines. In *The Listener*, David Pryce-Jones highlighted the recurring Big Brother theme in both works. Of *Private View*, he wrote, 'The rhythms and repetitions of the play, of course, are those of interrogation by the secret police. The odious pair are simultaneously cajoling and menacing: Ferdinand must remake himself in their image, or else. The suspense is cut through when he walks out on them. This, the two interrogators cannot stand ... His rejection leaves them to their own emptiness. Rather than face this, they would sooner crush and kill – in the danger, there is pathos, as Havel has the humanity to see.'[15]

Picking up on the head maltster's request for co-operation in *Audience*, Pryce-Jones wrote, 'Will Ferdinand help, and kindly inform on himself? This, then, takes farther the secret police parable of the first play. Guilty because the authorities declare him guilty, a man must still be able to furnish pretexts for that guilt ... The play reaches through to the insight that Ferdinand's nuisance value is also his protection against the state. It is the head maltster who is defenceless.'[16]

In *The Times*, Joan Bakewell found much to praise. 'In the hands of any other writer and actor, Ferdinand might come across as a prig and a phoney,' she wrote[17]. 'He does not. A performance of perfect control and naturalness from Michael Crawford makes him the one true man at the play's heart. Around him cavort hilarious grotesques: Ian Richardson and Zena Walker as the hollow couple, Freddie Jones as the confused man. Innes Lloyd produced, Claude Whatham directed. Everyone deserves credit.'

In 1979 Václav Havel was jailed for four years on charges of 'attempted subversion of the republic'. Ten years later, after another jail sentence, he led the Civic Forum movement to victory in Czechoslovakia's peaceful revolution. 'Truth and love must triumph over lies and hatred,' he told joyous crowds in Wenceslas Square, Prague.[18] On 29 December 1989 Havel became President of Czechoslovakia.

Crawford was seen in *Play for Today* after the first two episodes in the final series of *Some Mothers Do 'Ave 'Em* had already been shown. For many, it was as if the programme had never been away. The thirteen episodes from the first two series were constantly repeated, and Frank Spencer was kept alive by the mimicry of impersonators such as Mike Yarwood. It was exactly the programme the BBC needed in its battle with ITV for viewers at the end of 1978. The commercial channel had lured away two of its top acts, Morecambe and Wise and Bruce Forsyth. Now the BBC pitted *Some Mothers Do 'Ave 'Em* into the Saturday-night schedule against *Bruce Forsyth's Big Night* on ITV. It was broadcast in the middle of the evening's entertainment, which also included *Larry Grayson's Generation Game* and a new series of *All Creatures Great and Small*. Against ITV's big-money signing, the BBC scored a decisive victory, with all three programmes heading the TV ratings immediately[19]. *Some Mothers Do 'Ave 'Em* went straight into the chart at No. 1, with an audience of almost twenty million.

Between planning the series and recording it, producer Michael Mills moved to ITV, so Sydney Lotterby – whose comedy successes included *Porridge* – took over. Raymond Allen again wrote the scripts, this time from stories originated by Crawford, who was anxious to show Frank to be more mature – well, slightly. 'I knew that Frank had to grow up, after five years,' said the star[20], 'or he would seem a complete idiot. In this series he is more in command, but still getting things wrong – simply because he is accident-prone.' Certainly the character had a new confidence, and a new posh voice reserved for special occasions, but the calamities soon piled up.

The intended new departure was signalled in the first episode

113

with a move of house for Frank and Betty. Beginning with Frank directing removal vans and other vehicles, with inevitable results, it soon sees the couple's home of seconds earlier fall down as Frank disappears round the corner in the removal lorry. Then, as the driver struggles to keep pace with Betty, who is driving in front, Frank tumbles out of the back. Furniture is strewn down the road, but there is no sign of the hapless hero. Soon he surfaces from a vat of hot tar, covered from head to foot; the 'tar' was really food flavouring. It is not long before Frank is causing havoc in his new neighbourhood.

Clive James, whose *Observer* column had made him the doyen of television critics in the Seventies, wrote; 'One has been kept from previous series of *Some Mothers Do 'Ave 'Em* by its awful title, but it is time to say what everybody is saying – that the show is a must. Largely due to Michael Crawford's pertinacity in setting up his stunts and special effects, the slapstick is almost invariably funny. The level of language is high, too. "Did it have to come to this? Ejaculated from our fixed abode." It is fitting that a hero so maladroit should be a Malaprop as well. The central character is so consistently developed that the audience take it for granted the house will fall down only a few weeks after he has started [sic] to live in it.'[21]

It was only from looking at film of the first episode that everyone remembered Frank had forgotten to wear his famous beret and raincoat. They soon returned. As usual, there was no shortage of hair-raising stunts in the series. For the first episode, the house that crumbled was in a real North London street designated for demolition. In another story, Frank tries his luck as a gas repair-man and, while he is working in one house, there is an enormous explosion and the doors and windows blow out. Frank then walks out of the front door, covered in soot, and says, 'I don't think you should have any more trouble there. Good day!' That one line was an example of the writing and rewriting that made *Some Mothers Do 'Ave 'Em* such a success. 'Michael asked me to come up with a funny line for him to say on leaving the house,' recalled script-writer Raymond Allen[22]. 'I would write about forty, and he said to me once: "I always skip the first twenty because they're not very good!"'

One of Crawford's most terrifying stunts came when Frank took a job as a motorcycle courier. Naturally it results in acrobatics, with Frank driving through a tent – in which two people are sleeping – and speeding through a hay loft, leaping fifty feet through the air, crashing into a pond, then driving out of the water after being submerged. During his exploits, he was seen riding side-saddle and backwards. 'We used a motocross park at Dartford for Michael to get some experience,' said stunt arranger Val Musetti[23]. 'He does pick things up very quickly, and he is very keen to do it. It's something that has taken us years to do and he has to do it in five minutes.' For the mid-air leap, Crawford had to drive up a narrow thirty-foot ramp and jump from a height of seven feet over a wall. Musetti built a bed of boxes the other side to break his fall. 'I ordered about two thousand boxes,' he recalled[24]. 'The BBC went mad, but I said: "Would *you* like to do it? I would need about a quarter of the boxes, but I can't be sure where he is going to land. Would you take the chance?" I had the boxes four-deep and canvas on top.

'Michael was apprehensive about the leap and I said: "If you don't feel like it, I will jump on and do it." He said: "No, I'll have a go." I told him that when he came up the ramp he must accelerate on the throttle at speed so that he got the front wheel up in the air, so he wouldn't nosedive and hurt himself. I was on the other side with the boxes, waiting for him. Just before he reached the ramp, I could hear the engine hesitate; he throttled down. I shouted: "Open up the throttle." He opened it up at the last minute, came flying over and it was a terrific shot. I had taken him over two or three-foot ramp jumps beforehand, just for him to get the feeling. Maybe he had a little doubt as he approached the ramp, but he opened up the throttle again and landed on the rear wheel, as planned.'

For the next sequence, Crawford and the Suzuki had to jump into a pond; a three-foot ramp was used this time. The bike was sealed to make it waterproof and tracks were laid down under the water for it. This meant that Crawford would ride it out, appearing from under the water; divers with oxygen bottles enabled him to breathe.

The breathtaking stunts sometimes required others to put their lives in his hands. 'I was on the back of the motorbike on some shots,' said camera operator Rick Gauld[25]. 'He was a good driver and I trusted him implicitly. It was wonderful fun shooting the series, and Michael was great to work with. He is very meticulous and quite demanding, and hasn't got time for people who don't know their job.'

Similar acrobatics came into play for the last episode of the seven-part series, a forty-five-minute Christmas special in which Frank learns to fly. During the previous year, Crawford had himself learned the art of flying, near his new Bedfordshire home, in just seven weeks. At the same school, filming was done for Frank's less auspicious performance. Crawford had asked Raymond Allen to write an episode about this. The idea was that Frank was considering emigrating to Australia to help his grandfather – played by Dick Bentley, the original Ron in *The Glums* radio serial – to run his large sheep station, and the ability to fly would help enormously. As Frank takes to the skies in a light aircraft, his instructor collapses from a heart attack, and Frank bounces the plane off a road, sticks his leg out, spirals from 3,000 feet to a mere 250 feet, and narrowly misses the control tower.

Raymond Allen recalled that Crawford had flown to the Isle of Wight several times while they were planning the series. 'The first time,' he said[26], 'I was standing at Sandown airport and told this man that Frank Spencer was flying the plane that was coming down to land. He gathered his family together quickly and they rushed out of sight!'

When the third series of *Some Mothers Do 'Ave 'Em* ended, Crawford decided to hang up Frank Spencer's beret and raincoat for ever. Not even a five million-dollar offer from American television could persuade him to resurrect Frank. The offer, from ABC, came shortly after the last episode was screened and would have required him to make twenty-four programmes a year for a possible five years. Apart from not wanting to spend most of his time in America, Crawford felt that making so many episodes would sound the death-knell for Frank. He decided to kill of the beloved character while still at the height of his popularity. Staying in television, Crawford switched to ITV and found a new character.

Chapter 15

FATHERS, FLOWERS AND FANTASIES

Michael Mills, who produced the first two series of *Some Mothers Do 'Ave 'Em*, had moved to Thames Television and was making comedies for ITV. Crawford followed the exodus of BBC stars when he agreed to star in a six-part series, *Chalk and Cheese*, for Thames, to be produced and directed by Mills. The scripts were by newcomer Alex Shearer, on whose only previous television work it was based, a single half-hour comedy called *Spasms*. Broadcast in 1977, it centred on two expectant fathers – played by Jonathan Pryce and Robin Hawdon – in the waiting room of a maternity ward. Crawford took over the role of Dave Finn, and Hawdon continued as Roger Scott. The first episode of the series was effectively a re-run of the 'pilot'.

Chalk and Cheese described the difference between the two leading characters in the series, who become neighbours in the second episode, but it was also apt in the distinction between Dave Finn and Frank Spencer. 'Finn's the sort of bloke who is a randy, exuberant extrovert, whereas Frank Spencer is frightened of his own shadow,' said Crawford at the time[1]. 'There's nothing timid about Finn and, believe me, it's very refreshing playing an all-out extrovert for a change.' Complete with bushy beard, Crawford revelled in his role as the wild, unemployed, opinionated, loud-mouthed Finn, antagonist to trendy, clean-living, middle-class neighbour Scott. Michael Mills said, 'I see his new character as a younger Alf Garnett, loud-mouthed and cockney, but more rebellious and less reverent to authority. A sort of picket-line Garnett.'[2] Whereas Crawford had borrowed some of his daughter Lucy's characteristics for the role of Frank Spencer, here he used his soccer friend David Webb's habit of sticking out his chin and his driver's way of philosophizing about all and everything. No daring stunts were called for, except skidding in a four-wheel-drive limousine while working as a chauffeur in one episode.

The first episode received a mixed reception from TV critics. In the *Daily Express*, James Murray wrote, 'Mr Crawford's impressive acting skills leave not a trace of the gormless Frank – on the contrary – in the abrasive confident Dave Finn, know-all and man of the people.'[3] Richard Afton of the London *Evening News* felt that Finn *did* rely on the character of Frank Spencer and blamed producer Michael Mills, adding, 'But Crawford is too intelligent an actor to allow this to continue and, with his brilliance, it should develop into a highly successful series.'[4] Herbert Kretzmer, in the *Daily Mail*, summed up the dilemma:

ON THE evidence of *Chalk and Cheese*, it would seem that Michael Crawford is heartily sick of his old, adoring audience and wants no more of it.

His new TV character, unveiled last night, is a calculated assault on the cosy goodwill Crawford has built up over the years.

The character of Dave Finn in *Chalk and Cheese* is not even one you could grow to 'love to hate'.

Finn's manners, attitudes and apparel are those of an incorrigible, ramshackle, loud-mouthed dropout. It is an unrelenting portrait, defying affection, with few soft edges or compensating virtues. The role seems designed not only to bewilder Crawford's former followers, but actively to arouse their disgust.

The theme of last night's launch was childbirth or, more to the point, male 'phantom pregnancy'.

This may well be a fit subject for comedy, but Alex Shearer's script played it strictly for tactless slapstick that is bound to alienate even those who don't care either way for Crawford, but do share an old-fashioned respect for the dignity of birth.

We meet the messy, chirpy Finn in a maternity hospital awaiting his third child. He wears long hair, an earring, pyjama trousers and a beard. Sharing the bench is a smart, clean-cut, conventional young man awaiting his first child.

Finn's neurotic fancy is that it is not really his wife, but *he*, who is about to produce an infant. Busily knitting a pink toddler outfit, he talks and thinks like an expectant mother. 'This is my third,' he says and then, doubling up with labour contractions, gasps, 'It's getting near my time.' He proudly pulls up his shirt to reveal 'stretch-marks'.

The other father-to-be, though appalled by the uncouth Finn, is later persuaded to assist him through a simulated phantom birth which has Finn flat on his back groaning 'It's coming! It's coming!' while kicking his legs about in a grand display of distress and agony.

You have to admire Crawford's courage, if not his judgment, in thus testing his credibility and acceptability as an actor. And certainly the idea of coupling and contrasting a militant, dishevelled prole with an uptight Mr Clean is legitimate sit-com territory which might yet develop into an arresting and novel glimpse of the class war.

But last night's introductory episode will be seen by many as an affront not only to the sacred ceremony of birth, but also to women at large (no pun intended). An air of chauvinism sits heavily on the enterprise.

Both fathers, incidentally, are pictured as smug, self-esteeming, excitable and incompetent – two further images of ineptitude to swell the vast parade of male dimwits who already crowd the TV screens of Britain.[5]

Chalk and Cheese immediately went to No. 3 in the TV ratings during the spring of 1979, with almost seventeen million viewers. By the end of the series, it had lost one-third of them, many finding it difficult to adjust to Crawford's new television character. One who definitely did not like Dave Finn was his grandmother, who watched the programme with her back to the TV set and phoned friends and relatives to assure them that her grandson was nothing like that! Thames Television had thoughts of making a second series of *Chalk and Cheese* the following year, but Crawford eventually decided against it.

This was the beginning of an unsettled period for him professionally, as he searched for a new vehicle for his talents. Crawford was always most at home in the theatre, where he loved the rapport with a live audience, but his next stage musical, *Flowers for Algernon*, in London's West End, was an unmitigated flop. He was about to accept the starring role in another musical when director Peter Coe asked him to play Charlie Gordon in *Flowers*. Crawford agreed within twenty-four hours of receiving tapes of the show's music. Coe, artistic director of the Citadel Theater in Canada, had just staged the production there and had previously worked in London's West End with the English National Opera. Michael White, famous for staging shows such as *The Rocky Horror Show*, *Oh! Calcutta!*, *Annie* and *A Chorus Line*, was the producer of *Flowers for Algernon*, and Charles Strouse, composer of the *Annie* score, wrote the music.

Based on a novel by Daniel Keyes, the musical told the story of a mentally retarded man, Charlie Gordon, who has a 'miracle' operation to turn him into a genius, but he slowly reverts to his childlike state. The same treatment has already been given experimentally to a mouse called Algernon, and Charlie sees what will happen to him as the mouse slowly deteriorates into idiocy.

It was an ambitious subject for a musical, and Crawford was utterly devoted to it, describing it as the most challenging role of his career. He prepared for it by visiting mental hospitals and talking to doctors and patients. He also remembered a man called Sam who swept up and did odd jobs in his stepfather's grocery shop in Kent when he was a child. Sam was mentally handicapped and lived in a nearby home, and the work gave him an independence that would otherwise have been difficult for him to find. 'He was a lovely man, kind and gentle,' recalled Crawford[6], 'and you could see the bewilderment in his eyes at trying to cope with a world that went too fast for him.' This musical was very close to the star's heart, and for years afterwards he would describe it as the best work he had ever done in the theatre, despite its failure to attract audiences.

Preparing for the show also meant Crawford had to overcome his fear of mice. The title role went to a white mouse, and there were four of them ready to tread the boards. In one scene, the mouse had to run up and down Crawford's sleeve as he sang and danced. Playing the teacher with whom Charlie falls in love was Cheryl Kennedy.

Flowers for Algernon opened at the Queen's Theatre, London, on 14 June 1979 and reviews were generally good; certainly there was no hint of what was to come. B.A. Young wrote in the *Financial Times*, 'It is unconventional, but it contains an intrinsic advantage. Michael Crawford, potentially an outstanding young actor, has chosen to specialise in playing retarded boys or young men for years, and a musical with a retarded young man as the hero was just the thing ... I thought it all charming, once Mr Crawford was out of the moron stage. "Good, but simplistic," Charlie says about *Jekyll and Hyde*. He might say it about *Flowers for Algernon* if he were sitting in the stalls. Simplistic isn't a bad thing for a musical to be.'[7]

When Crawford's grandmother went to see the show, once again she made her presence felt. At one point, Crawford had to ask Cheryl Kennedy, 'Did I do good?' Edith Pike stood up and shouted, 'Oh, Michael, darling, you did better than good.'[8] The audience roared with laughter, but she was not finished. When Cheryl Kennedy asked, 'Any questions?' she was on her feet again, hand in the air, saying, 'Yes, I've got a question. How did you all learn your lines so quickly?' Everyone took her interruptions with good humour, and the star laughed until the tears flowed. Those were tears of happiness, but sadness soon followed.

After the show's first ten days, producer Michael White told a stunned cast that the musical would close at the end of four weeks. Audiences were not big enough to cover costs, which were so high in London's West End as to demand immediate returns. New VAT rates on theatre tickets and hotel and restaurant bills were blamed, and other productions were already beginning to feel the pinch. Another show, Alan Ayckbourn's *Joking Apart*, closed shortly afterwards, just four months after its opening, ending hopes of a long summer run. Faced with closure, Crawford and the cast of *Flowers for Algernon* offered to work for nothing, such was their belief in the musical, but they were told that would not be enough to save it. An original-cast album was released in America, in the hope that the show might still get a chance there, but it was not to be. Cliff Robertson had won an Oscar for his lead role in *Charly*, a 1968 American film version of the story.

Bewildered by the show's closure, Crawford took another break. '*Flowers for Algernon* was more demanding and more satisfying than anything I've ever done,' he said a year later[9]. 'I was heartbroken when it folded and went round the world on holiday to get over the shock.' Aware of the need to pay daughters Emma and Lucy's school fees, he also revived Frank Spencer in a TV commercial for Texaco petrol. He is seen as the passenger in a Morris 1000, being driven by an old lady, and is holding a kite out of the window. Suddenly he gets sucked out of the car and lifts off into the air, before falling, at which point the commercial finishes with a 'freeze-frame' of him in mid-air. Stunt arranger Marc Boyle, who worked with Crawford on *Some Mothers Do 'Ave 'Em*, advised him here. 'We wired him to a helicopter,' recalled Boyle[10]. 'That took him into the air, about 250 feet up, but you never saw it in the commercial. It was quite a hairy stunt. Then, to see him fall, he had to jump about thirty-five feet from a big crane on to an airbag, which was to break his fall.'

Back at his Bedfordshire cottage, Crawford looked after his three acres of land, and the chickens and geese, and made jelly and piccalilli.

When he started work again, it was in a film for Walt Disney Productions, *Condorman*. He starred as Woody Wilkins, an American cartoonist who turns his fantasies into reality by trying out the feats attempted by his comic-book character Condorman. Soon he is in the cloak-and-dagger world of international espionage, delivering secret documents to a beautiful Russian spy – played by Barbara Carrera – in Turkey as a favour for a friend who is a filing clerk with the CIA in Paris. He uses the codename Condorman and is later hired by the CIA to assist in the same KGB spy's defection; he agrees to do so if the intelligence organisation will build all Condorman's gadgetry for his next adventure. Woody meets Natalia, the Russian agent, in Yugoslavia and a series of car and boat chases follows. More than anything, it was a spoof of the James Bond films.

Based on the novel *The Game of X* by Robert Sheckley, *Condorman* was directed by British-born Charles Jarrott, who was then living in France and had just made the film *The Last Flight of Noah's Ark*, another Disney 'real-life' adventure. *Condorman* was made on location in France, Monaco and Switzerland during some of the worst weather Europe had experienced for years.

Colin Chilvers, who won an Oscar for his visual effects on

Superman, was responsible for *Condorman*'s special gadgets, such as a walking stick that turns into a machine gun, a laser cannon and seven pairs of Condorman's wings. He was also behind the explosions that blew up six large boats and six Porsche 935 Turbo Carreras.

The wings donned by Crawford had a diameter of twenty-two feet. Unfortunately the flying sequences were not very impressive, especially when judged alongside those in *Superman*. Here the wires could occasionally be seen in the 'live' shots, and studio close-ups superimposed against real backgrounds were not very convincing. Colin Chilvers' other special effects were also left wanting compared with the new generation of action films that had grown up since *Star Wars*. Disney bosses had invested fourteen million dollars in the film, and they got what they paid for.

For the first time in his professional life, Crawford was not allowed to do all his own stunts. Disney figured that in scenes where he was wearing his birdman-like Condorman outfit, complete with mask, people would not be able to see his face anyway, so why risk the star's life? Even then, although stuntman Conin Skeaping stood in for parts of the flying routines, Crawford did other parts of the hazardous sequences himself.

He terrified director Charles Jarrott by standing on the edge of the Eiffel Tower, 300 feet up; worse followed. A crane suspended Crawford by wires for the film's opening flying scene, but no one had anticipated the strong current in the River Seine, where he had to crash-land and be dragged through the water by an unseen launch. 'I rehearsed it meticulously – as I always do with every stunt – but things went terribly out of control,' he recalled[11]. 'The wings began to sink, dragging me underwater. For the first time in stunt work, I was really frightened. I honestly believed I was going to cop it. Luckily for me, the film crew rescued me.'

In lighter moments, Jarrott made fun of Crawford in his yellow Condorman outfit. 'He was very embarrassed standing there in his tights, with those wings on,' said Jarrott[12]. 'I used to tease him and call him Tweety Bird.' Much of the time, the director was trying to persuade the star that he simply could not do the stunts called for in the film, but Crawford had his own way more often than not. At one point Woody Wilkins had to hang suspended 200 feet above the Alps on a cable two-thirds of the way up the Swiss Matterhorn.

'I planned to do a few feet of Michael shooting up the cable, then put a stuntman in,' said Jarrott[13]. 'He was most unhappy about this. In the end I had to do a private deal with him. I would let him go about 3,000 feet and photograph it in such a way that it could only be him doing it. We fixed a wire to the cable to make it safe. He loved it – I've never seen him so happy.'

Colin Chilvers designed a self-propelling jet rod to carry Crawford up the cable in Zermatt. He was presented with bigger problems when a motorboat chase almost went disastrously wrong. One of the boats, loaded with explosives and fuel in preparation for a controlled explosion, ripped loose and headed at high speed straight for another boat containing the film crew, who froze with horror. At the last moment, it switched course, headed for a marina where boats worth half a million pounds were berthed, finally veered off in another direction and hit a cliff, exploding in the process. Only minutes earlier, thirty spectators had been standing there; fortunately Chilvers had had the foresight to remove them.

Apart from his Condorman outfit, Crawford was dressed as a gypsy and a Bedouin during his attempts to rescue Barbara Carrera. It was a semi-spectacular film, with its beautiful locations, daring stunts and colourful costumes, but it would have been more at home in the Sixties when spy thrillers and spoofs were at their height. It could hardly compete with the gadgetry and special effects that were becoming commonplace in box-office hits such as the *Star Wars* and 'Indiana Jones' films of the late Seventies and early Eighties. They, too, were aimed primarily at children but did not expect to get away with short-changing their audience.

Despite these shortcomings and the bad weather, fun was had making the film. 'One of the particular pleasures about this film was the lunch breaks,' said Charles Jarrott[14]. 'It's one of the great pleasures about working on location, particularly in France. They make lunch an event, and it creates an absolutely marvellous ambience and mood among the crew that lingers over the production the rest of the day. Very rejuvenating. Lunch starts when the last man leaves the set; you sit down at a table with tablecloth, a little wine, good conversation.'

Oliver Reed, who played an evil KGB agent, had very few scenes with Crawford but found, during lunch breaks, that he had changed little since they made *The Jokers* almost fifteen years earlier. 'I would always order the most expensive things on the menu, such as smoked salmon and caviar,' recalled Reed[15], 'and say to the waiter: "Michael Crawford has asked to pay for this," and Michael would scream: "No, I didn't. No, I didn't." While filming, I would lock him in the make-up room, go on to the set and shout: "Where's Michael?" He was a great one for playing practical jokes on!'

When *Condorman* was released in 1981, reviews were lukewarm. Trying to find some good points in it, the *Daily Mail*'s critic remarked that 'happily, there's always Crawford, who exudes an energy and enjoyment in what he is doing that are sufficiently infectious to make a visit to *Condorman* worthwhile'[16]. *Variety* believed it had 'the look and depth of a 15-year-old episode of television's *Wonderful World of Disney* series'[17].

The film was a disappointment, as so many Disney productions had been since its founding father, Walt Disney, died in 1966. Lack of imagination and a sense of purpose were the company's biggest problems, but that was to change when new management took over in the Eighties, creating the Touchstone Pictures label and making films such as *Who Framed Roger Rabbit* and *Good Morning Vietnam*, re-establishing Disney as one of the world's top entertainment organizations.

During the period in which he made *Chalk and Cheese*, *Flowers for Algernon* and *Condorman*, Crawford was also lacking a sense of purpose. His greatest success, Frank Spencer, had become a millstone round his neck. His decision to ditch the character was to be admired and, professionally, entirely correct, and it was perhaps inevitable that he would go through an unhappy transition before finding another popular success that would also satisfy his energetic, creative yearnings.

Chapter 16

BARNUM

When Crawford was offered the role of the great nineteenth-century American showman Phineas Taylor Barnum in a new London musical, it signalled the start of a decade of uninterrupted stage success that would see him become an international star. It was something he had been close to before but never quite attained. Producer Harold Fielding took him to see Jim Dale, another British all-round entertainer, starring in the New York version of *Barnum*, the circus musical that had then been running almost a year. Once certain changes had been agreed, Crawford accepted the title role in the British production and was determined to add more spectacular circus skills to those seen on the Broadway stage.

In January 1981, he set off for six weeks' training at the New York School for Circus Arts, where he learned all the tricks and, importantly, how to fall properly. On his first day there, he spent fourteen hours working and soon settled into a routine of at least four hours' training a day.

The circus skills that Crawford began learning less than six months before *Barnum*'s opening at the London Palladium were ones that most big-top entertainers learn as children. 'When Michael Crawford first came here,' said Paul Binder, artistic director of the New York School for Circus Arts[1], 'we knew something of his reputation, but we tend to look askance at reputations, not because we don't admire somebody's work in the theatre but, when they come here, they have got a whole lot of other kind of work to do, an absolute need for concentration, dedication, hard work. You can't fake it when you work on circus tricks. In the theatre, they have a thing called "motivation for the actor"; we say in the circus that motivation is "you miss the trick, you break your neck".

'From Day One, he made it clear that he was going to work as hard or harder than anybody was asking him to. He was spending four and five and six hours a day, and a good deal of that time was on his own, after instruction. Michael would absolutely refuse to leave until he got what he was looking for out of the piece of work that he was working on for that day.

'None of us take it lightly and, unless a stranger, an outsider, comes in taking it as seriously or more seriously than we do, we tend to want to shut them out. We have worked with six or seven stars of *Barnum* around the world. Michael, by far, was the most dedicated of them. I wouldn't say that he has the more innate talent than any one of them, but his absolute refusal *not* to take the next step – he had to take the next step every time.'

Crawford returned to London and continued to practise his newly acquired skills in the lonely isolation of a community hall in Kennington. He had limped back from New York with an injured leg and back as a result of his falls – and he already had calloused feet from walking on the high wire. On his first day on the wire, his feet had bled, but he soon mastered the art, ready for his twenty-foot walk ten feet above the Palladium stage.

'I'm not really good at anything, at all these skills,' said Crawford[2]. 'I am competent. You must sell them, though, with great pride. That's what I *was* taught. Whatever you achieve – if you're juggling with three balls – it's enormous pride that you've done it. Well, as you're learning and you actually do achieve the skill of juggling three balls, your face is just glowing and you watch every member of the company, their face, and you go: "Look, look, look at me." That you must never lose; that's something that you have to do every night at the end of every trick you present.'

Meanwhile, 1,180 people were being auditioned to find twelve with skills that would complement those being learned by the show's star. For Crawford, it was the most physically demanding role of his career, and he said he would not regret a moment of his gruelling training even if the show flopped, as had *Flowers for Algernon*, whose director, Peter Coe, teamed up with Crawford again for *Barnum*. They need have had no worries about the spectacular musical failing to draw audiences, but there was a scare when the acrobatic star was rushed to the Nuffield Clinic, in Hyde Park, two weeks before the show's official opening. The strain of rehearsing sixteen hours a day suddenly took its toll, and Crawford arrived for a final dress rehearsal weak and unable to stand up straight. He was suffering from nervous exhaustion and was ordered to take four days' rest, with no visitors to his hospital bed. Four previews of *Barnum*, due to start the following day, were cancelled. When he rejoined the cast after his short break, Crawford explained, 'I always push myself too far. This time, I pushed myself even further. I wasn't sleeping or eating properly. I lived on sandwiches and junk food instead of steaks. I should have been eating in proportion to the energy I was using. Now, I'm one-and-a-half stone below my normal weight. I'll be having good, healthy meals and vitamins from now on.'[3] A day later, he was back on stage for the first of the remaining eight previews.

The physical demands of his role had struck him down at about the same time as the emotional strain of splitting up with girlfriend Jo-Anne Robinson, whom he had met when she was a dancer in the musical *Billy*. Love blossomed when they worked together again in the ill-fated *Flowers for Algernon*, in which she was assistant choreographer. As they grew closer, she wanted to marry, but he preferred to keep their relationship as it was. Eventually she walked out on him. Two days later he phoned and said he would marry her, but she said it was too late. Shortly afterwards, the dancer wed Australian actor John Diedrich, the star of a London revival of the Rodgers and Hammerstein musical *Oklahoma!*, in which she also appeared, at the Palace Theatre. A year later, Crawford was finding comfort in the arms of Jane Watts, a dancer in *Barnum*. He had always admired dancers. 'I prefer them to actresses,' he said[4]. 'Actresses are always flicking their hair back. Dancers are a very physical breed. They are usually gritty, earthy people.'

The success or otherwise of *Barnum* depended almost totally on Crawford. It was *his* show, although the contribution of every member of the cast was never underestimated; they helped to make it the spectacle that it was. Members of the audience were greeted by a stilt-walker outside the theatre and clowns in the auditorium, creating the atmosphere of a circus even before the show began.

The boxes on each side of the stage were used for parts of the show, so, for the first time in the Palladium's seventy-year history, they were closed to the public[5].

Because of the dangerous stunts, the £600,000 musical was insured for five million pounds, three million of that to cover its star. It was the most highly insured show in British theatre history[6]. During the preview performances, one of which was attended by Princess Margaret, Crawford suffered a painfully bruised heel after a fall from the top of a model house went wrong, but nothing was going to stop him from making it through to the first night on 11 June 1981.

His months of hard work and total dedication paid off with a triumphant first-night performance, which showed again that a thin story in a musical was almost an obligatory ingredient for Crawford to show off his breathtaking skills and capture the hearts of the whole audience. As the first act neared its end, he took to the high wire, singing as he stepped across it. At one point he wobbled dangerously and it looked as if he would fall. 'Then,' he said[7], 'the Angel of the Lord came down and lifted me from above. It's what's known in the trade as a miracle.' He had been a little unsettled by the installation of a new wire, looser than the previous one, which had collapsed the night before; but he made it across the tightrope and even members of the orchestra applauded.

Towards the end of the show, Crawford made his final entrance – after a mysterious disappearance of almost two minutes – sliding down a rope from the highest reaches of the Palladium. It was a daring feat that caused producer Harold Fielding to go white and silent for several seconds when the star had originally told him of his intention to add this to the version of *Barnum* they had seen together on Broadway. During his absence from the stage, Crawford had to run through the Palladium's corridors at speed, taking eighty-five steps in twenty seconds, change into a ringmaster's outfit, step on to a platform high above the stage, attach a safety strap to his right hand and slide down the rope. It was a fitting climax to this theatrical spectacular, and that first-night audience gave Crawford an eight-minute standing ovation, calling him back as many times. He had never experienced such a sensational reception.

Actor Robert Morley, one of many celebrities who watched that first performance, said, 'In fifty years in the theatre, I've never seen anything like it.'[8] Crawford returned home from the first-night party to hear the eight-minute standing ovation reported on the radio, staying awake to hear the news again and again, taking in the magnitude of his new success. In the morning he read with glee the newspaper reviews. The *Daily Mirror* headlined it 'The greatest show in town' and critic Ken Irwin wrote that Crawford's was 'a performance so brilliant, it's impossible to top', adding[9], 'It's a long time since I've seen an audience go away so happy. And if you don't go home singing and believing there's still some joy in the world, then you ain't got a heart.'

Michael Coveney of the *Financial Times* put the performance into perspective. He wrote:

Barnum's the name and humbug's the game. So announces Michael Crawford before laying claim to the title of sole remaining copper-bottomed musical theatre star of today.

The show that has proved a Broadway triumph for Jim Dale comes fully equipped with all the right prerequisites: feeble book by Mark Bramble, indifferent lyrics by Michael Stewart and corny music by Cy Coleman. Anything more would have been disastrous. The whole thing works a treat and succeeds in blowing clean through any critical bogusness I am capable of mustering.

The Barnum technique is clearly exposed in his ability to transform the misfired exhibition of the oldest woman in the world, Joice Heth, into a box office hit by labelling her, with scant regard for historical accuracy, 'George Washington's nanny'. At this point the stage erupts in a company cakewalk you could only resist by filling your boots with lead and contemplating the Middle East crisis.

The construction of the American Museum (where Barnum could only get more people through the turnstiles by beguiling the clientele with a view of an 'Egress') is beautifully staged in *One Brick at a Time*, with bricks flying all over the place and Mr Crawford applying the cream with a tweak of subtle dexterity. Well into the show by now, the most spectacular thing he has done is to spin a coin.

Black and white – as we see in the second act imposition on

respectable Bridgeport of a riot of streamers, balloons and circus acts – has no real place in the Barnum philosophy. Hokum and colour are all that count. When the Swedish Nightingale, Jenny Lind, arrives in the delectable shape of Sarah Payne, she not only lives up to her title with a fine display of soprano coloratura, but also threatens Barnum's marital stability.

The first act closes with Mr Crawford delivering a storming number as he crosses the stage on a tightrope to the singing Swede's private box. The book, magnificently lousy, now reveals its one real surprise quality, narrative and theatrical restraint. After the interval, the show bursts forth again with an invasion of the auditorium by a marching band. The sudden decline into Barnum's various disasters is just as suddenly halted by the lure of the Big Top. The Greatest Show on Earth is saved for the finale, Mr Crawford shooting down from the auditorium's highest point on a long rope to join the jugglers, acrobats and sequinned American totems.

Also worth watching out for are Jennie McGustie as a delightful stomper and Tom Thumb (Christopher Beere) dancing along in the shadow of Jumbo the Elephant with a pair of beefeaters on enormous stilts.

The audience responded with the most spontaneous standing ovation I have seen in a London theatre. Even allowing for First Night hysteria, you sensed that the home of variety, and Michael Crawford, deserved nothing less.[10]

Soon *Barnum* was almost the only London West End show to challenge the spectacle of the Andrew Lloyd Webber hit musicals *Evita* and *Cats*. It was clear that the circus-based musical would run and run, depending on Crawford's energy. In *Punch* magazine, Sheridan Morley highlighted a side to the star's performance that explained why *Barnum*'s London stage life was so dependent on him. 'What makes Crawford considerably more fascinating in the role than was Jim Dale on Broadway,' he wrote[11], 'is that he retains the very real possibility of failure. Every moment of the show therefore becomes a cliff-hanger; whether intentionally or not he gives the constant impression that his entire circus may be about to fall apart at the seams of the big top, and when it doesn't the mixture of relief and exultation that spreads first across his face, then across the stage and finally out into the auditorium becomes a wave of sheer theatricality the like of which you will find nowhere in town or country. Where Jim Dale's Broadway Barnum is a ringmaster in constant command, Crawford's is more like a circus-struck teenager who has suddenly been given the uniform and told to try it for size.'

Six months after *Barnum*'s opening, Crawford was named Actor of the Year in a Musical in the Society of West End Theatre Awards. There was more to celebrate a month later when he turned forty and the cast gave him a champagne party at the Palladium after the previous night's performance; daughters Emma and Lucy were there, too. Then it was announced that the show's run would be extended to February 1983. Ronnie Corbett and Ronnie Barker were due to play a summer season of *The Two Ronnies*, but they did just four weeks in June 1982 – while the *Barnum* cast took a much deserved rest – and returned eight months later. Crawford holidayed in Crete, where he went wind-surfing and mono-skiing, during the cast's short break.

Showing off his athletic skills every night was energy-consuming and, following his illness before the show's opening, he was looking after himself much better. During each performance, he would drink two-and-a-half litres of mineral water and take plenty of salt, to compensate for all the body fluid he was losing on stage. He tried to maintain his $9\frac{3}{4}$-stone weight by eating bacon and egg for breakfast, a large steak, potato and salad for lunch, and lamb chops with two vegetables for dinner, although that diet sometimes went astray and he hoped that taking plenty of vitamin pills would keep up his strength.

By the time it ended its run in February 1983, *Barnum* had been performed 663 times, breaking Danny Kaye's record for the Palladium's longest-running show. After the last performance Crawford slumped on to the large black sofa in his dressing-room, surrounded by toy clowns, gifts from fans. After twenty months in the role of P.T.Barnum, he could begin to wind down and take it easy, and in March 1983 he had the satisfaction of seeing British ice-skating duo Torvill and Dean perform a routine based on *Barnum* during the world championships in Helsinki, which they won.

The skaters, British and world champions, had become interested in a circus theme after Dean watched the state circus in Moscow and thought it would provide the novelty and originality they sought in their performances. The couple went to see *Barnum* at the Palladium, and Crawford invited them to his dressing-room afterwards. Enthusiastic about the idea, he and the show's music director, Michael Reed, offered their services free. Some of the show's musicians also contributed by playing for a session in a recording studio. Crawford, in gym shoes, took to the ice to show the pair how to mime juggling and other circus tricks for their four-minute free-dance routine. Torvill and Dean performed it for the first time during the British championships in 1982.

Everyone knew that *Barnum* could have run and run at the London Palladium, and the star had no intention of letting the character die. He remembered the words of Evelyn Laye, who had appeared with him on stage in *No Sex, Please – We're British*. 'Never turn your back on success,' she told him[12]. So, in the middle of 1984, he prepared to revive *Barnum* for an eighteen-week run at the Opera House, Manchester, which had been a bingo hall for the previous five years and was returning to its intended role for the £750,000 production.

First, he returned to the New York School for Circus Arts, followed by television producer-director Alan Benson, who was making a half-hour film for *The South Bank Show*, ITV's acclaimed arts series, presented and edited by Melvyn Bragg. 'Melvyn and I were walking past the Palladium one day,' recalled Benson[13], 'and Melvyn said: "We should do something about Michael Crawford." It's legendary how willing he is to do things that involve him in personal risk and, in digging around a bit, I found out this business about him going to the circus school. We filmed him on his last night at the Palladium and, trying to think of something interesting to do, we said to Michael: "Why don't we take you back and go through some of the things you learned and also get you to learn some new things?" He agreed and we contacted the circus school and found his trainer, Sacha, who was the sort of person who would jump off a fifty-storey building with no safety net. "It's just technique," he would say.'

Some of the new skills that Crawford learned were never used in the show. Alan Benson persuaded him to try flying the trapeze, but the musical's insurance would never allow him to do so on stage.

'Michael had never done a trapeze jump before,' said Benson[14], 'and he was terrified. There was a point at which I was thinking: "We won't do it." He did do it, but he said afterwards it was absolutely horrific.'

A spectacular new skill that Crawford was able to use in the show was where he dangled by one hand from a rope that was twirling, its speed increasing to thirty-five miles per hour. He called it the Human Milkshake and explained, 'The G Force is terrifying. My clothes would be dragged off if I didn't have such big feet.'[15]

Back in Britain, Crawford trained at the Hillingdon School of Gymnastics, in Middlesex, and attained such high standards that he was awarded a British Amateur Gymnastics Association badge and certificate as a qualified coach.

However, his exhilaration at bringing new life to the clown Barnum was marred on the first morning of rehearsals for the Manchester production by the death of his beloved grandmother, three months short of her ninety-ninth birthday. Earlier that year, she had been in Bedford General Hospital with a chest complaint, and her famous grandson did an impromptu show for the patients while visiting her, bringing plenty of laughs to everyone. She recovered but died in the same hospital in August 1984.[16]

Since his mother's death, his 'Nan' – and, later, daughters Emma and Lucy – had meant more to him than anyone else. Whenever he returned to his Bedfordshire cottage, she had been there waiting, often with undecipherable telephone messages, a legacy of the failing eyesight she suffered in later years. Now she was gone, and the man who put all his energy and devotion into his own stage performances, determined never to be beaten, needed the support of the closely knit Barnum cast to pull him through the days and weeks after his grandmother's death.

'It was hard – very hard,' he recalled[17]. 'She was the best friend I've had. She was simply everything to me. I even built her a place next to my cottage so that we could be together; she meant so much. My only consolation is that I was there with her when she went. We were holding hands as she died.' The following year, on what would have been her one hundredth birthday, Crawford held a special party in memory of his dear grandmother.

By then, Barnum was wowing audiences again as if it had never been away. In Manchester it had become the first provincial show

Barbra Streisand was the star of Crawford's first Hollywood film, *Hello, Dolly!* Here the pair help Danny Lockin to his feet after taking a fall while dancing.

Crawford and wife Gabrielle leave Heathrow Airport for New York to attend the première of *Hello, Dolly!* After a promising start in cinemas, audiences fell dramatically and Twentieth Century-Fox was battling for its survival.

Daughters Emma (left) and Lucy remained a link between Crawford and his wife Gabrielle after the couple split up. Eventually, the girls' parents forged a new friendship, but there was no newly found romance between them.

Emma (left) and Lucy, grown up and proud of their father, celebrate with him after the opening of *The Phantom of the Opera* in New York. American critics' scathing remarks about the musical's content were tempered by their praise for Crawford's performance.

Actress Janet Mahoney watches as Crawford dives through a serving hatch, one of the pieces of slapstick he performed nightly on stage in *No Sex, Please – We're British*.

The black beret and Army raincoat were the trademark of Crawford's most successful TV character, accident-prone Frank Spencer in *Some Mothers Do 'Ave 'Em*. Michele Dotrice played his long-suffering wife, Betty.

Crawford and stunt arranger Derek Ware hang on for their lives as window-cleaning stunt for *Some Mothers Do 'Ave 'Em* goes disastrously wrong. After twenty minutes dangling high over London's North Circular Road, they were pulled to safety.

Another terrifying stunt, during the last series of *Some Mothers Do 'Ave 'Em,* saw Frank Spencer taking a job as a motorcycle courier. After causing mayhem on the streets, he sped through a hay loft and a pond.

Above: a bearded Crawford and co-star Cheryl Kennedy prepare for the ambitious musical *Flowers For Algernon.* It closed after only four weeks and Crawford sadly described it as the most satisfying work he had ever done.

Above: the fantasy world of Billy Liar gave Crawford another starring role on the London West End stage. Critics raved at his performance and hailed him as the West End's newest star.

Below: Crawford dons his wings to rescue Barbara Carrera in his role as Woody Wilkins in the Disney film *Condorman.*

Singing and treading the high wire at the same time were not demanding enough for Crawford in his physically exhausting role as Barnum, so he added a spot of juggling. The show ran, on and off, for five years.

Crawford reached new heights of success in *The Phantom of the Opera*, alongside Sarah Brightman, and stunned audiences with his operatic tenor's voice.

to take one million pounds in advance bookings, and during its run Crawford was given a special Variety Club of Great Britain lunch in his honour at the Piccadilly Hotel, Manchester. Remarkably, he then took the musical back to London's West End, where it opened at the Victoria Palace Theatre on 14 March 1985, with its insurance cover increased to £7,600,000. A couple of months later, Prime Minister Margaret Thatcher was there to see it, and meet its star afterwards, and on 9 September Crawford made his one thousandth appearance as Barnum.

The BBC made a television film of the stage show, which was screened at Christmas 1986, eight months after the show finally closed. Producer Harold Fielding had no doubts that it could have run for at least another year but had no intention of featuring another star once Crawford had hung up his clown's outfit after 1,210 performances. The show belonged to Crawford and, after five years, he felt that he had given his all to the circus musical. In all those performances, he had fallen off the tightrope no more than a dozen times, a remarkable feat for one not born into the circus, but his feet were scarred for life. During the recording of the BBC's £1,400,000 TV production, Crawford fell off the tightrope four times and was not best pleased, but it was all right on the night. Several months after the show finished, he also found that he had bursitis in his shoulder as a result of his rope-spinning trick. His new professional dilemma was how to follow up such a fantastic success, but first he planned a long rest. He was never very good at not working and soon found himself launching into a role that would take him to even greater heights of fame.

Chapter 17

THE PHANTOM

When the curtain finally came down on *Barnum*, Crawford treated himself to a two-week holiday in Saint Lucia but came back after only six days. He had planned to do no more theatre for a couple of years and concentrate on television and films, but he found an offer to star in a new Andrew Lloyd Webber musical, *The Phantom of the Opera*, irresistible. While in Saint Lucia, he was on the phone to the composer almost daily and eventually decided he just had to return to Britain.

Andrew Lloyd Webber was the undisputed king of the British musical. Over the previous fifteen years he had enjoyed London West End successes with shows such as *Jesus Christ Superstar*, *Evita*, *Tell Me On a Sunday*, *Cats*, *Song and Dance* and *Starlight Express*. Their popularity was increasingly a result of the package presented to audiences: two or three good tunes, highly dramatic theatricals and stunning sets. No matter that the tunes were unoriginal and the stories lacked substance. After he split up with his early collaborator, lyricist Tim Rice, Lloyd Webber worked with various wordsmiths. He ran his own company, The Really Useful Group, and his empire included ownership of the Palace Theatre, in London's West End.

In 1983 Lloyd Webber divorced his first wife, Sarah Hugill, by whom he had a son and a daughter, and married Sarah Brightman a year later. She had made her name in the raunchy dance group Hot Gossip, who came to fame on television in *The Kenny Everett Video Show*, and was lead singer for their Top Ten hit single, *I Lost My Heart To a Starship Trooper*. She met Lloyd Webber when she was a dancer in his show *Cats*, based on T. S. Eliot's poems, and was chosen by him to sing in the première of *Requiem*, a 1985 version of the Latin Requiem Mass. As a singer, her range and sweetness of voice were marred by a constant, affected vibrato and one-dimensionality of tone. Lloyd Webber never agreed with her critics and saw *The Phantom of the Opera* as a musical totally suited to her voice, writing the lead role of Christine Daaé to accommodate her wide vocal range.

The original novel, written by Frenchman Gaston Leroux and published in 1911, was inspired by a visit to the Paris Opera House. Leroux was fascinated by the cellars and passages of the building, which had once been a prison, and saw the possibilities for developing a character who could haunt the Opera House and disappear into its secret depths. He wrote about a masked musician, whose face is hideously deformed, being besotted with a young soprano of the *Opéra Populaire* and exerting a hold on her. While writing *Le Fantôme de l'Opéra*, Leroux remembered a horrific accident there in 1896 when one of the chandelier's counterweights fell on the audience, and he decided to build this into the story. 'The Opera ghost really existed,' he wrote in the introduction to his book, setting up what was intended to be a gripping tale.

On publication the book made little impact, but the story was resurrected by Universal Pictures in Hollywood, which had already enjoyed film success with *The Hunchback of Nôtre Dame*. Its star in that classic, by Victor Hugo, was Lon Chaney, who was then cast as the Phantom, again playing a disfigured hero who worships the young heroine. Universal spent one million dollars on this 1925 silent film, building a five-tier replica of the Paris Opera House interior and hiring three thousand 'extras' for crowd scenes. It is still regarded as the best film version.

Less successful was an attempt by Universal to reissue the film as a 'talkie' in 1930, shooting a few dialogue scenes, poorly dubbing the heroine's singing voice, and adding music. Leroux had died three years earlier, but his story was to remain popular with film producers for the rest of the century. Universal made another version, starring Claude Rains, in 1943; it won Oscars for cinematography and art direction. Here the Phantom was overshadowed by the opera itself, with much of the $1,750,000 budget spent on musical sequences, singers and lavish costumes.

A 1960 Mexican version, *El Fantasma de la Opereta*, projected the Phantom as someone to be feared by every chorus girl. The chilling theme continued two years later in a British production, by Hammer Films, starring Herbert Lom. A variation on the theme came in a 1974 American spoof, *Phantom of the Paradise*, a massive flop more noteworthy for the fact that Sissy Spacek was the set decorator than anything else[1]. An American TV movie of the same year, *Phantom of Hollywood*, set the story in a film studio. Another TV movie, in 1983, switched back to the original title and featured Maximilian Schell, Jane Seymour and Michael York.

The story's potential in the theatre had not really been exploited, although David Giles adapted and directed a 1975 Actors' Company production in London starring Edward Petherbridge, Sharon Duce and Keith Drinkel, and, in 1984, Ken Hill staged a spirited version at the Theatre Royal, Stratford, East London. Hill had approached Sarah Brightman to play Christine but she declined because of other commitments. When Andrew Lloyd Webber saw a newspaper review of this production, he telephoned theatre producer Cameron Mackintosh, who had staged *Cats* and *Song and Dance* with him, and mentioned the idea of making a new musical out of *The Phantom of the Opera*, to which Mackintosh warmed. The two watched the Lon Chaney and Claude Rains films, then went to see Ken Hill's stage production.

At this point there was no thought of Lloyd Webber writing a new score; the magnificence of contemporary music by Delibes, Massenet and Gounod would feature in this new version. It was intended to be like *The Rocky Horror Show*, whose director, Jim Sharman, was approached to make the new *Phantom* production. He said he was not available but suggested that the show needed a romantic storyline and that Lloyd Webber should compose new music for it. When Lloyd Webber and Mackintosh both found copies of the original novel, they discovered in the story the romantic elements that had been missing from previous productions. For the first time the composer had found the plot for a love story, which had always been his ambition; he saw this as his *South Pacific*.

Hal Prince, who had made *West Side Story*, *Cabaret*, *Evita* and many more hit musicals, agreed to direct, and Richard Stilgoe started work on the story. Lloyd Webber sought someone to write the lyrics, and approached Alan Jay Lerner, who had written *Brigadoon* and *My Fair Lady*, but he was too ill and died shortly afterwards. Tim Rice was also asked, but he was busy with his own musical, *Chess*[2]. The composer then approached little-known Charles Hart, who had been highly commended in the Vivian Ellis Musical Writers Competition. Lloyd Webber, Stilgoe and Hart drew on elements of romance in the Leroux novel and adapted the story to give it the greatest dramatic effect, losing or changing parts in the process.

It was while picking Sarah Brightman up from a singing lesson with teacher Ian Adam that Lloyd Webber had heard Crawford performing and been impressed by his vocal range. Rock singer Steve Harley, who sang with Brightman on the hit single of the musical's title song, which had already been released, hoped to play the lead role, but the composer wanted Crawford and approached him two days after it was announced that *Barnum* would finish its stage run. Crawford was enthusiastic and returned early from his holiday in the West Indies to prepare for the role.

In August 1986, rehearsals began at a hall in Kennington, South London, under the direction of Hal Prince and distinguished choreographer Gillian Lynne. Crawford's preparations were already well under way. There were none of the physically challenging stunts for which he was normally acclaimed, but there were a few tricks, such as falling through a trap door in the stage.

Crawford's biggest challenge was to develop his voice into that of an operatic tenor, and he did this with the same dedication that he usually gave to putting his life at risk. 'With the help of my singing teacher, Ian Adam, I knew I could do it,' said Crawford[3]. 'It was difficult at first, but then Andrew realized that he could get me to use every single note coming out of my upper level – then using two octave singing so that you have the low range, and the upper registers are utilised as well to terrific dramatic effect.' He practised five hours a day, using his diaphragm to give his voice the required sound. As usual, there was a physical cost; this time his chest muscles expanded, putting added strain on the rest of his body.

There was also the discomfort of wearing the make-up for the Phantom's disfigured face, designed by Christopher Tucker, who had previously helped to disguise John Hurt for *The Elephant Man*. Layers of latex were applied to Crawford's face; then two wigs were fitted, together with a radio microphone to pick up his voice, followed by two contact lenses, one blue and one milky white; and, lastly, the Phantom's vertical half-face mask was added. This process took Crawford and make-up artist Tiffany Hicks three hours every day, although they eventually reduced it to two hours; it took the best part of an hour to remove. Before the make-up was applied, Crawford's face had to be moisturized and his hair wetted down; his face was also shaved. Wearing the latex and the wig proved to be very uncomfortable and limited what he could do. While made up, Crawford could not eat properly; on days with matinée performances, this lasted twelve hours. He quickly learned to drink tea and soup through a straw.

Crawford was reputed to be earning several thousand pounds a week, plus seven-and-a-half per cent of the box-office receipts and a percentage of the profits even after he eventually left the London production. The £2,000,000 musical already had advance bookings worth £250,000 before it was announced that Crawford would star in it; during the following month they rocketed to £600,000, justifying Lloyd Webber's decision to feature a star whom some people considered a surprise choice. Apart from his musical hits, Crawford could point to the fact that, as a teenager, he had starred in Benjamin Britten operas. Now he was working on his vocal skills to make his light, airy singing voice stronger; the results on the show's original-cast album – which went straight to No. 1 in the LP charts[4] – were impressive, but he made even further strides as the show's success snowballed over the next few years.

The Phantom of the Opera was due to open at Her Majesty's Theatre, in London's West End, on 9 October 1986. The final matinée preview performance was cancelled when Sarah Brightman suffered a throat virus, but she was back for the first night. It was Crawford's night. Amid general critical praise, with reservations about the musical's schmaltz, he was once again credited with taking a production on to a plane above that deserved by its content.

Under the slightly misleading headline 'God's gift to musical theatre', Irving Wardle of *The Times* pointed out that Gaston Leroux's story provided all the ingredients needed for a stage spectacular. 'Some of these opportunities have been seized by Andrew Lloyd Webber and his collaborators, and projected with stunning showmanship in Harold Prince's production,' he wrote[5]. 'But their full range has been much restricted by the decision to present the events above all as a tragic love story.' Although that was the mainspring of Leroux's plot, contended Wardle, much of the story's vitality depended on the jokes played by the Phantom on the opera's staff and wretched managers. Charles Hart had produced love lyrics in 'saccharine abundance' and the work soon became monotonous, with 'risible pastiche' as a substitute for nineteenth-century opera.

In the *Daily Telegraph*, John Barber balanced the shortcomings in the musical's substance against the lavish presentation. He wrote:

OUTBURSTS of sudden applause, and a standing ovation at the end, paid tribute to the soaring ballads and the sensational stage effects in Andrew Lloyd Webber's *The Phantom of the Opera* at Her Majesty's. The reception was understandable, indeed deserved, although the substance of the work is unmitigated tosh.

But it is tosh of a high order and of peculiar interest. It is based on Gaston Leroux's often-filmed story about a girl obsessed by a demon lover. This is yet another of those enduring myths which erupted from the erotic repressions and night fears of the late 19th century, like Stevenson's *Jekyll and Hyde*, Du Maurier's *Trilby* and Bram Stoker's *Dracula*.

A team of supreme theatre craftsmen have seized avidly on its lush romantic agony to produce a musical as sumptuous and unashamedly stagey as a Victorian pantomime – a blessedly trad antidote to the current craze for shows chock-ablock with laser beams, video screams [*sic*] and fake holographs.

The master showman Harold Prince has taken seriously a melodrama which risks audience laughter at its overwrought and unlikely exaggerations. Thanks to his tactful treatment that laughter never comes ...

Michael Crawford is superb – tense, controlled, tigerish – as the mystery man, conjuror, musician and murderer who terrifies the Opera personnel into thinking him a ghost. Hideously deformed beneath his mask, he appears behind mirrors to a minor singer, Christine, and Svengali-like he mesmerises her to a stunning command of coloratura and top B-flats.

In one thrilling episode, he steps through the mirror and leads the terrified girl down, down into the Opera's vaults and pilots her, Charon-like, across the subterranean lake below to his abode there, lit by a thousand candles. 'Sing! Sing!' he cries, attired as a Chinese mandarin and madly playing a handy, if unlikely, pipe-organ.

And sing she surely does. Owing her career to the monster, you watch her gratitude being eaten into by fear. Sarah Brightman makes a remarkable West End debut with her choirboy-pure, wide-compass voice and rhythmic sense of melody. More: although tall, her bone-thin dancer's figure and baby face endow Christine with just the right naivety and fragility for a girl duped – practically doped – by music. Irrelevantly but irresistibly, a line sung by the Phantom – 'Since I first saw you, I needed you to sing for my music' – recalls that she is the composer's wife ...

Lloyd Webber revels in parodies of the superannuated gilts of Victorian opera – a sadist whipping chorus girls round an Aida elephant on a gaslit stage encrusted with gilt cherubs, breaking into a glorious quarrel-septet [sic] and climaxing in a masquerade which loads the famous staircases with teaming dancers choreographed by Gillian Lynne.

Two sickly, gorgeous but overweight melodies (good lyrics by Charles Hart), *The Music of the Night* and *All I Ask of You*, will I suspect become standard. I came out torn between two feelings: admiration for the colossal nerve it took to mount a show so preposterous without guying it; and awareness that the composer, in yet another attempt at something new, sometimes strained his musical gifts beyond their reach. But, if only the phantom of a true opera, this is as spectacular a piece of true theatre as London has seen in years.[6]

Michael Coveney of the *Financial Times* described how the musical's melodramatic story and lavish presentation reached a crescendo, in a way that would spellbind audiences and ensure sell-out performances for years to come. He wrote:

Andrew Lloyd Webber's new musical opens quietly, with an

142

auction of properties at the Paris Opera House: a musical monkey, a broken chandelier. The story of the phantom is alluded to, the furniture undraped and the gilded Opera proscenium revealed. A riotously colourful dress rehearsal of *Hannibal* is in progress as two new managers survey the scene. An elephant comes on. The chorus girl Christine Daaé is part of the background to Carlotta's aria, which sounds Meyerbeer-ish.

It is a stunning opening sequence in an evening that restores sex and romance to the modern musical, with a full quota of pulsating melodramatic tension as Christine is possessed by the opera ghost, abducted to his subterranean lake and torn between the needs of a freak and the loyalty of her childhood sweetheart Raoul, the Vicomte de Chagny.

The music maintains several linking motifs and miraculously covers a range of 18th and late 19th century operatic pastiche and lushly orchestrated ballad owing much to Lloyd Webber's admired Richard Rodgers while preserving its own distinct, idiosyncratic sound.

The composer worked in the first place with librettist Richard Stilgoe and the distancing prologue reflects their return to the Gaston Leroux novel: the key point is that Christine, devoted to the memory of her dead musician father, receives the phantom at first as her father's messenger, his angel of music, and misreads that function as a lover's overture.

In Leroux, Raoul overhears their latest encounter in a dressing room. That scene becomes the show's sensational launching pad, Michael Crawford's half-masked phantom materialising in the mirror and leading Sarah Brightman's entranced Christine to his candle-lit lake. The title number, with its panoply of descending rock chords and augmented seconds, bursts open. The couple disappear in a trap and then (thanks to sleight-of-hand doubling) emerge in flight at the top of the proscenium – the stage is now the sewer, the gondola the bridal bed, the great portcullis a barrier against the world and its opera managers, prima donnas and second-rate composers ...

The final moments, as Christine rips off the mask and the

lovers' triangle is resolved in a descent to the lair and an emotional farewell, are almost unbearably moving. You would be well advised to have the Kleenex handy.

This, I have to say, is due not just to the power of the music, which gathers irresistibly, but to the performance of Michael Crawford, reasserting his pre-eminence as the outstanding star of our musical theatre. There is nothing flashy or grotesque here: an ordinary man in a beautiful white mask has a facial deformity but sings like an angel. Crawford measures his gestures and emotional leaks to perfection, humiliated and mortified when Christine rips off his Fu Manchu mask, devastated when she returns the ring and departs, as he would wish, with Raoul.

Miss Brightman needs to submit more to this spellbinding appropriation, but she reveals again a bell-like, cultured soprano that moves easily between rock and operatic idiom, rising smoothly to a top B-flat. Steve Barton's loyal Vicomte is a little too lined and wooden as yet. The best support comes from Rosemary Ashe's technically virtuosic and poisonously put-out Carlotta, and from John Savident and David Firth as the new managers and Mary Millar as the dancing mistress Mme Giry.

The work of new lyricist Charles Hart is more than promising. Gillian Lynne has staged the musical numbers with some finesse. The musical direction of Michael Reed is exemplary.[7]

Crawford was thrilled with the critical acclaim for his performance, but even more so with the reactions of his daughters. Lucy, then eighteen, was there for the first night and was so stunned by what she saw and heard that there were tears in her eyes as she approached her father afterwards and whispered in his ear, 'I just didn't know you could do that ... had that in you.'[8] She had difficulty getting the words out, and the two were soon sobbing. It had been the same when Emma attended a preview performance, unable to speak coherently after the show and phoning her father later to tell him how overwhelmed she was.[9]

It was daughter Emma who had to push him from his seat at the Laurence Olivier Awards two months later, when his legs felt numb after he was named Best Actor in a Musical. At the same ceremony, *The Phantom of the Opera* was proclaimed Musical of the Year. Awards continued to come, with Crawford being voted the Variety Club of Great Britain's Showbusiness Personality of the Year and the show named Best British Musical in the Ivor Novello Music Awards.

Then Crawford had to pay the price of the physical demands he had made on his body to develop an authentic operatic tenor's voice. In April 1987, when Sarah Brightman left the show after fulfilling her six-month commitment to it, Crawford collapsed with a hiatus hernia, known as 'singer's hernia'. He was ordered by doctors to rest for at least ten days and Steve Barton, who played Raoul, took over as the Phantom. On his first night, Barton injured a knee while falling through the trap door on stage. Crawford realized that Barton, who was also a dancer, could ruin his career if he continued with a damaged knee, so the star left his private hospital bed after just a day to return to the stage. Audiences at the matinée and evening performances that day were expecting to be told that Crawford was unable to appear, but theatre manager Ray Mansell was able to announce before the shows that Crawford was back. That night he won a ten-minute standing ovation, but he was under heavy medication throughout both performances and doctors examined him every time he left the stage, telling him that he was bleeding internally. After the evening performance Crawford went back to the Cromwell Hospital, in South Kensington, and was told the following day that he had aggravated his hiatus hernia and only complete rest would cure it. His second understudy, James Paterson, a former member of the Scottish Opera, stood in as the Phantom until Crawford returned two weeks later, doing just six instead of eight performances a week at first.

The ultimate accolade came when Crawford was awarded an OBE in the Queen's 1987 birthday honours list. Daughters Emma and Lucy accompanied him to Buckingham Palace, where the Queen enquired about his health and told him that the honour was being made in recognition of all his work, not just for *The Phantom of the Opera*. Royalty had long been among his fans: the Princess of Wales and the Duchess of York had both been to watch him as the Phantom, and shortly afterwards the Queen Mother met him, expressing horror when Crawford peeled off his mask to reveal the character's grotesque face.

Prime Minister Margaret Thatcher also went to see the show. In the audience at the same performance was Colin Graham, who had directed Crawford in the Benjamin Britten productions *Let's Make an Opera* and *Noye's Fludde*. He was now artistic director of the Opera Theater of St Louis, in America, and could not hide his pride at how the star's talent had flourished in the thirty-two years since they had first worked together. 'I didn't go backstage afterwards,' he said[10], 'because I knew Mrs Thatcher was there and it would be busy. I went home and called him that night, hoping he would still be at the theatre, and he was. It was so wonderful because, after all those years, he was just the same Michael on the telephone and he was clearly delighted that I'd been delighted, and he was genuinely humble and appreciative of what I said.'

Crawford left the London production after a year and had a two-month break before opening in *The Phantom of the Opera* on Broadway. During that time, he recorded an album of some of his favourite musical numbers, called *Songs From the Stage and Screen*, backed by the London Symphony Orchestra[11]. 'I thought it was a remarkable record,' said Colin Graham[12]. 'He had worked so hard on the voice and it was such a beautiful album, and still had all Michael's personality on it. I haven't heard him sing without a microphone, but I class him along with Barbra Streisand. The actual singing and the technique used to put over the numbers is impeccable.'

Jonathan Pryce had reportedly turned down the chance to take over from Crawford as the Phantom in London – ironically, Crawford had previously taken over Pryce's starring role in the 'pilot' episode of the TV comedy series *Chalk and Cheese* – and the part went to Dave Willetts, who had been in the original cast of *Les Misérables*, before taking over the lead role of Jean Valjean from Colm Wilkinson[13]. Claire Moore, who had stood in for Sarah Brightman during some performances took over the role of Christine when she left in April 1987. Brightman returned for a month just before Crawford handed over to Willetts the following October, then the two original stars prepared for their starring roles in the New York production.

Chapter 18

PHANTOM TAKES FLIGHT

Crawford denied reports that he would earn £1,000,000, including two per cent of box-office takings, for his nine-month run on Broadway, but he was certain to be a very rich man at the end of it. Andrew Lloyd Webber had battled hard so that the actors' union, American Equity, would allow Sarah Brightman to play Christine in New York; it had originally opposed the idea, saying that Crawford was the musical's only British star of international stature, but it eventually agreed to the appearances of both Brightman and Steve Barton, as Raoul, in return for two American actors appearing on stage in Britain.

After a holiday in the Bahamas, Crawford began rehearsals in New York in December 1987, working more than eight hours a day before returning to a fifty-fourth-floor apartment on West 57th Street with a spectacular view of Central Park. That Christmas, alone in the city, was rather like the one he had spent twenty-one years earlier, before opening in his only previous Broadway production, *Black Comedy*. This time, daughters Emma and Lucy had given him a surprise turkey dinner before he left Britain.

For Christmas Day itself, Crawford bought a chicken, vegetables and an expensive bottle of red wine, and put nuts and sweets out on the table. He switched on the oven, only to find later that it was not working. Then he took the oven apart, in a scene that must been reminiscent of Frank Spencer in *Some Mothers Do 'Ave 'Em*. Eventually he put the chicken in a small toaster oven, but the result was rather pitiful. This time in New York he began to feel more a part of the city and his loneliness soon disappeared.

The Majestic Theater had taken a record $22,000,000 in advance ticket sales[1] and was almost totally booked for the length of Crawford's run, but the star – still on medication to relieve the pain of his hiatus hernia – had yet to face the first-night critics, known as 'the butchers of Broadway' because of the enormous influence they had on a show's success, on 26 January 1988. Reviewers in Britain had expressed their reservations about the extreme grandeur of the Lloyd Webber show, but in America they were to launch a full-blooded attack on the eight million-dollar production. Fortunately for Crawford, they recognized the strength of his performance and found it one of the show's few qualities to commend.

Frank Rich, whose *New York Times* column makes him the most powerful theatre critic in America, wrote:

It may be possible to have a terrible time at *The Phantom of the Opera*, but you'll have to work at it. Only a terminal prig would let the avalanche of pre-opening publicity poison his enjoyment of this show, which usually wants nothing more than to shower the audience with fantasy and fun, and which often succeeds, at any price.

It would be equally ludicrous, however – and an invitation to severe disappointment – to let the hype kindle the hope that *Phantom* is a credible heir to the Rodgers and Hammerstein musicals that haunt both Andrew Lloyd Webber's creative aspirations and the Majestic Theater as persistently as the evening's title character does. What one finds instead is a characteristic Lloyd Webber project – long on pop professionalism and melody, impoverished of artistic personality and passion – that the director Harold Prince, the designer Maria Bjornson and the mesmerizing actor Michael Crawford have elevated quite literally to the roof. *The Phantom of the Opera* is as much a victory of dynamic stagecraft over musical kitsch as it is a triumph of merchandising uber alles.

As you've no doubt heard, *Phantom* is Mr Lloyd Webber's first sustained effort at writing an old-fashioned romance between people instead of cats or trains. The putative lovers are the Paris Opera House phantom (Mr Crawford) and a chorus singer named Christine Daaé (Sarah Brightman). But Mr Crawford's moving portrayal of the hero notwithstanding, the show's most persuasive love story is Mr Prince's and Ms Bjornson's unabashed crush on the theater itself, from footlights to dressing rooms, from flies to trap doors ...

The physical production, Andrew Bridge's velvety lighting included, is a tour de force throughout – as extravagant of imagination as of budget. Ms Bjornson drapes the stage with layers of Victorian theatrical curtains – heavily tasseled front curtains, fire curtains, backdrops of all antiquated styles – and then constantly shuffles their configurations so we may view the opera house's stage from the perspective of its audience, the performers or the wings. For an added lift, we visit the opera-house roof, with its cloud-swept view of a twinkling late-night Paris, and the subterranean lake where the Phantom travels by gondola to a baroque secret lair that could pass for the lobby of Grauman's Chinese Theater. The lake, awash in dry-ice fog and illuminated by dozens of candelabra, is a masterpiece of campy phallic Hollywood iconography – it's Liberace's vision of hell.

There are horror-movie special effects, too, each elegantly staged and unerringly paced by Mr Prince. The imagery is so voluptuous that one can happily overlook the fact that the book (by the composer and Richard Stilgoe) contains only slightly more plot than *Cats*, with scant tension or suspense. This *Phantom*, more skeletal but not briefer than other adaptations of the 1911 Gaston Leroux novel, is simply a beast-meets-beauty, loses-beauty story, attenuated by the digressions of disposable secondary characters (the liveliest being Judy Kaye's oft-humiliated diva) and by Mr Lloyd Webber's unchecked penchant for forcing the show to cool its heels while he hawks his wares ...

Aside from the stunts and set changes, the evening's histrionic peaks are Mr Crawford's entrances – one of which is the slender excuse for Ms Bjornson's most dazzling display of Technicolor splendor, the masked ball (*Masquerade*) that opens Act II. Mr Crawford's appearances are eagerly anticipated, not because he's really scary but because his acting gives *Phantom* most of what emotional heat it has. His face obscured by a half-mask – no minor impediment – Mr Crawford uses a booming, expressive voice and sensuous hands to convey his desire for Christine. His Act I declaration of love, *The Music of the Night* – in which the Phantom calls on his musical prowess to bewitch the heroine – proves as much a rape as a seduction. Stripped of the mask an act later to wither into a crestfallen, sweaty, cadaverous misfit, he makes a pitiful sight while clutching his beloved's discarded wedding veil. Those who visit the Majestic expecting only to applaud a chandelier – or who have 20-year-old impressions of Mr Crawford as the lightweight screen juvenile of *The Knack* and *Hello, Dolly!* – will be stunned by the force of his Phantom.

It's deflating that the other constituents of the story's love triangle don't reciprocate his romantic or sexual energy. The icily attractive Ms Brightman possesses a lush soprano by Broadway standards (at least as amplified), but reveals little competence as an actress. After months of playing *Phantom* in London, she still simulates fear and affection alike by screwing her face into bug-eyed, chipmunk-cheeked poses more appropriate to the Lon Chaney film version ...

Thanks to the uniform strength of the voices – and the scaring, Robert Russell Bennett-style orchestrations – Mr Lloyd Webber's music is given every chance to impress. There are some lovely tunes, arguably his best yet, and, as always, they are recycled endlessly: if you don't leave the theater humming the songs, you've got a hearing disability. But the banal lyrics, by Charles Hart and Mr Stilgoe, prevent the score's prettiest music from taking wing. The melodies don't find shape as theater songs that might touch us by giving voice to the feelings or actions of specific characters.

Instead, we get numbing, interchangeable pseudo-Hammersteinisms like 'Say you'll love me every waking moment' or 'Think of me, think of me fondly, when we say goodbye'. With the exception of *Music of the Night* – which seems to express from its author's gut a desperate longing for acceptance – Mr Lloyd Webber has again written a score so generic that most of the songs could be reordered and redistributed among the characters (indeed, among other Lloyd Webber musicals) without altering the show's story or meaning ...

Yet for now, if not forever, Mr Lloyd Webber is a genuine

phenomenon – not an invention of the press or ticket scalpers – and *Phantom* is worth seeing not only for its punch as high-gloss entertainment but also as a fascinating key to what the phenomenon is about. Mr Lloyd Webber's esthetic has never been more baldly stated than in this show, which favours the decorative trappings of art over the troublesome substance of culture and finds more eroticism in rococo opulence and conspicuous consumption than in love or sex. Mr Lloyd Webber is a creature, perhaps even a prisoner, of his time; with *The Phantom of the Opera*, he remakes La Belle Epoque in the image of our own Gilded Age. If by any chance this musical doesn't prove Mr Lloyd Webber's most popular, it won't be his fault, but another sign that times are changing and that our boom era, like the opera house's chandelier, is poised to go bust.[2]

David Patrick Stearns of *USA Today* also had praise for Crawford but contempt for the production as a whole. He wrote that it lacked the scope of *Les Misérables* and the emotional depth of Stephen Sondheim's latest musical, *Into the Woods*, and declared, 'In the end, the phantom saves the opera … what keeps this wobbly blockbuster from collapsing under its own grandeur is Michael Crawford. His characterization of the disfigured phantom terrorizing a Paris opera house galvanizes the show into grand theater – for the last 20 minutes. Only then does *Phantom of the Opera* live up to its staggering hype, which no work of art should have to withstand.'[3] Stearns was critical of the 'hyper-romantic score' and 'well-dressed comic-book characters', adding, 'Much of this doesn't matter when Crawford is on stage. Though performing behind a mask, he projects a beguiling combination of danger, eroticism and anguish.'

The New York Times saw the need to reappraise the musical, but the verdicts were roughly the same. A day after Frank Rich's stinging review, Bernard Holland asked American composers: 'What is the music of Andrew Lloyd Webber's *Phantom of the Opera* worth?'[4] William Bolcom said, 'It's a lot like operas written in the late 17th century. Can you really extract the music of Cavalli from all those cherubs and wires and machines and make it stand on its own? I don't think so.' He added, 'In Verdi, the first court of appeal is the music. In Lloyd Webber it's just part of the show. In the circus, you want just the right music for the elephants, but it's the elephants you're meant to watch.'

Opera singer Frederica von Stade, who 'adored' *The Phantom of the Opera*, said, 'I thought the portrayals of opera were very human and loving – in fact the show itself seemed to me opera in its most accessible state.' Beverly Sills, head of the New York City Opera, also liked the show. 'It's a different art form than *Oklahoma* and *South Pacific*, and maybe more sophisticated,' she said. 'You really have to pay attention; there's more here than special effects. Also there's very little dialogue as there was in the old musicals.'

Composer Ned Rorem was acid in his appreciation of the score. 'The hype surrounding *The Phantom of the Opera* centers almost exclusively on its unprecedented financial success,' he said. 'Nobody mentions the poverty of its score. Despite Andrew Lloyd Webber's vast fortune, I can't think of any serious composer who would change places with him.'

Critic Walter Kerr weighed in more than two weeks later, broadly agreeing with his colleague Frank Rich. 'Let it be said, though, that Michael Crawford, as the Phantom, suddenly demands absolute attention in the show's final, desperate moments, making a fine thing of his ultimate emotional surrender,' wrote Kerr[5], who added, 'But in the end *The Phantom of the Opera* can be no more than the sum of its pictorial effects. It's not opera (not with those bland melodies, not with lyric phrases like "Be My Guest" and "Make My Night"), it's not a display case of serious acting, it's not humour (not even self-mockery). It's psychologically lightweight, long on melodramatic grotesquerie, and it can only live on its visual chills. Will three chills, plus candles that swarm like fireflies, do you?'

Newsweek magazine was rather more kind. '*Phantom* is shameless in its appeal to our most atavistic taste for melodrama, spectacle, *Grand Guignol*, sheer, blessedly silly fun,' wrote Jack Kroll[6]. '... The best part of Lloyd Webber's score is the purely romantic, indeed erotic, group of songs – *Angel of Music*, *The Phantom of the Opera*, *The Music of the Night* – centered on the relationship between the Phantom (Michael Crawford) and Christine Daaé (Sarah Brightman). These songs, with their reaching, yearning, impassioned melodies, are the most effective Lloyd Webber has ever written.'

Of the first-act sequence where the Phantom spirits Christine through her dressing-room mirror, down into his underground lair, Kroll wrote, 'Michael Crawford's performance here, and everywhere, is greatly compelling in its passionate sincerity and courageous emotional abandonment. His tenor voice rings through his half mask with desperate power as he handles the spellbound Christine like a human cello. And when he is unmasked he rivals Lon Chaney in his demoniac anguish.'

Whatever the critics said – and much of the criticism about the show's content was certainly on target – The Phantom of the Opera was a hit on Broadway. For that first-night performance, Crawford climbed two rungs higher on the ladder from which he leans out high over the audience, just to give himself a small extra challenge, literally to keep himself on his toes.

Daughters Emma and Lucy were the centre of attention at a champagne party afterwards, as photographers took pictures of them joyously hugging their father. Crawford's former wife, Gabrielle, was also there to see his triumph but kept a low profile after the show and declined to be interviewed. 'I was there to support him,' she said[7]. 'I was not there to steal anyone's thunder or take anything away from the production – which, if you start hanging around your ex-husband, is something you might be accused of.'

Gabrielle had split up with former Chelsea footballer Tommy Baldwin, by whom she had two sons, and was beginning to find success as a professional photographer, in addition to running her clothes shop. A year earlier, actress Jane Birkin – a friend – had asked her to take the stills photographs for her latest film and was so pleased with the results that she asked Gabrielle to do the same for her forthcoming concert tour.

When Gabrielle was seen with her ex-husband in New York, British newspapers speculated that they would remarry, but the couple quickly scotched the rumours. 'It always amazes me that people find it so strange that we're still friends,' said Gabrielle shortly afterwards[8]. 'He phones from New York at least twice a week and if he's in England we always have Christmas together – and to me it's so natural. But to assume I'm going to get married to him just because I see him and I go to first nights ...'

Three months after *The Phantom of the Opera* opened on Broadway, there was more press intrusion into Crawford's private life when a British Sunday newspaper revealed that his 'secret' daughter, Angelique, had made him a grandfather[9]. Angelique, the daughter of Crawford's former lover Patricia Mansell, from whom he had parted more than twenty years earlier, had married window cleaner Martin Conroy in 1986 and given birth to a son, Liam, in November 1987[10]. They lived in a rented, £22-a-week council flat in South London. Hounded by reporters in New York, Crawford resolutely refused to talk about it.

More happily, he was collecting a string of awards resulting from *The Phantom of the Opera*'s phenomenal success. The New York Outer Critics Circle named him Best Actor in a Musical and the show Best Musical; he won the same award from the New York Drama Desk, which honoured Hal Prince for his direction and split the Best Musical award between *The Phantom of the Opera* and *Into the Woods*, Stephen Sondheim's latest show. Then came the crowning glory when the Lloyd Webber musical won seven Tony awards; it took the Best Musical honour, Crawford was named Best Actor in a Musical, Hal Prince won the award for Best Director – his sixteenth Tony – Judy Kaye was named Outstanding Featured Actress in a Musical, Maria Björnson won awards for both Best Scenic Design and Best Costume, and Andrew Bridge took the one for Best Lighting Design. *The Phantom of the Opera* was even eclipsing the success of another British musical on Broadway, *Les Misérables*, which had won top honours the previous year.

Accepting his award at the Minskoff Theater, New York, Crawford told the audience, 'There are so many ups and downs in this business. By the law of averages, I am due to be knocked down by a truck. I would like to thank Andrew Lloyd Webber for choosing me.' Lloyd Webber, collecting the Best Musical award, took the chance to snipe back at the critics, especially for the way in which they had dismissed Sarah Brightman's performance. 'I thank you,' he said. 'I am deeply honoured. This is rather unexpected. And thanks to Sarah.' He looked in his wife's direction and she smiled back. At the same time, Brightman – who was not even nominated for a Tony – left the show a month early to work with the Berlin Philharmonic Orchestra; as in the London production, she had been booked to appear for six months. Crawford continued until September 1988 and, although missing Britain, agreed to star in a Los Angeles production the following year. As with *Barnum*, he was not going to turn his back on success.

After leaving the Broadway production Crawford took a break, during which he made a Christmas Day programme for British television intended to raise money for the Save the Children Fund. Filming included a trip to Africa, but by the following spring he was back in America, this time at the Ahmanson Theater in Los Angeles, where he would appear as the Phantom for eleven months. It was to become the most successful stage show in American West Coast history.

Crawford gained ten pounds during his New York run but lost it all within days of opening in Los Angeles. This time, he was the only British member of the cast; Dale Kristien was starring in the original Sarah Brightman role, and Reece Holland played Raoul. *The Phantom of the Opera* opened at the Ahmanson Theater on 1 June 1989 and the reception was much the same as in New York: enthralled audiences, and critics who panned the musical but praised Crawford. Dan Sullivan wrote in the *Los Angeles Times*:

Some of you may recall the strange affair of *The Phantom of the Opera*, a mystery never fully explained. How a sumptuous, but rather pokey, musical could sweep the field in London, New York and, now, Los Angeles, on the strength of one image – a little ivory mask.

Clever marketing doesn't totally explain the phenomenon. Nor does the fact that Andrew Lloyd Webber wrote the score, or that Michael Crawford is the star. Phantom has been a hit since the day it was announced. As Lady Bracknell used to say, the very title has vibrations.

A haunted opera house. A shadowy figure in the flies. A beautiful, mesmerized soprano. Monsieur, this is as far as I dare go. Monster, prepare to meet thy fate! Christine, over here!

Delicious. And we got it all at the Ahmanson on Wednesday night, plus the underground grotto, plus the 'plunging' chandelier (a fairly slow plunge), plus a lot of opera jokes. There was plenty to take in. But did we care?

Clearly, we were supposed to. *Phantom* has a lot of fun sending up the junk operas of 100 years ago, with their prop elephants and pudgy tenors ...

But *Phantom* is perfectly serious about its phantom, whom Michael Crawford plays even more quietly and intensely at the Ahmanson than he did on Broadway ...

This is dank, yeasty stuff – underground stuff that music can get at, if it goes deep enough. Faced with a similar challenge in *Sweeney Todd*, Stephen Sondheim got at some of it. Lloyd Webber simply doesn't have the tools or, perhaps, the persistence.

[Sullivan described the show's tunes as 'elevator music'.]

... *Phantom* would get four stars from any restaurant critic in the business for its 'presentation'. But it is serving Campbell's Tomato Soup ...

No one could accuse Michael Crawford of giving a canned performance. Crawford's crepuscular voice and his lynx-like moves do stir sympathy for our poor benighted Phantom, and you have to respond to his commitment as a performer – he couldn't give more to his part if it were written by Dante.

Crawford's Phantom combines size and intimacy in a way that only a very experienced musical theater performer could achieve. He comes close to us, and yet he brings off the grand gesture. The final renunciation scene is especially well-judged. Almost, he makes us believe ...

Prince's staging is impeccable, and the great set pieces flow like a film ...in the end, this *Phantom* suggests the story of the Emperor's Nightingale – beautifully jewelled, exquisitely sung and without a heart.[11]

Again, the critics' attacks did not stop the musical continuing to be a sell-out for months in advance. After Crawford eventually left the cast on 28 April 1990, handing over to Robert Guillaume – who played the butler in the American TV comedy series *Soap* and *Benson* – the show's average weekly ticket sales dropped slightly, from $711,000 to $705,000, but that was still big money and, within two months of Crawford's departure, *The Phantom of the Opera* became the biggest financial stage success Los Angeles had ever known.

During his eleven months on stage in the city, Crawford – to his surprise and slight embarrassment – was dubbed Hollywood's newest sex symbol and offered endless film roles. Wary of jumping at such offers and making a mistake, he was glad to savour his success as the Phantom before planning far ahead. He also remembered his previous trip to Hollywood, to make *Hello, Dolly!* more than twenty years earlier, and the way his film career had faltered after three disappointing pictures for Twentieth Century-Fox. 'You make a couple of bum movies and, for this town, that's it,' he said[12]. 'I slunk off home with my tail between my legs.'

Crawford led a relatively quiet existence in Los Angeles, renting a small apartment in the downtown area of the city. Each night after the show, he would come off stage soaked in sweat and drink a pint of Guinness, something he had been doing since the London production opened, because it contained much needed iron. Then, he would eat a meal, usually sticking to a Chinese herbal diet, which helped to cleanse his system and remove toxins. Crawford's hiatus hernia meant he had to look after himself, so there was no Indian food and rarely red meat; he also had a regular session of Shiatsu massage. For exercise he would cycle along the seafront or rollerskate on the Boardwalk at Venice Beach.

When Crawford finally bowed out of *The Phantom of the Opera* in Los Angeles, doctors ordered him to rest his voice for six or seven weeks; the technique he had used to project it to such great effect was straining his vocal chords. There were other physical aches and pains, too, brought on by running around the stage, appearing at great heights and leaning out, displaying the peculiar body movements demanded by the story. The construction of the Ahmanson Theater's stage made this more energy-consuming than in London and New York.

After 1,069 performances as the Phantom, Crawford took a short break, driving across America with daughter Lucy, before returning to Britain to start preparing for a planned film version of *The Phantom of the Opera*. There was other film and television work lined up, but he also intended to use his new position as an international star to help UNICEF, the United Nations Children's Fund.

Chapter 19

SAVING THE CHILDREN

It was Crawford's role as the vulnerable Frank Spencer in *Some Mothers Do 'Ave 'Em* that first made him popular with children, and he received frequent invitations to visit hospitals. He soon discovered the happiness he could bring to youngsters who were away from their parents or battling bravely against illness, perhaps reflecting on his own emotionally unsettled childhood and the loss of his mother when he was only twenty-one.

The star sometimes arranged for sick children to attend his stage shows. One such girl was eight-year-old spina bifida sufferer Dawn Harding, who watched him in *Billy* more than twenty times from her wheelchair; he frequently visited her in hospital, where she underwent numerous operations. Crawford also encouraged members of his fan club to write to Dawn. The fan club was another means of raising money for the needy; donations and money for signed photographs bought an ambulance for spina bifida children.

During *Barnum*'s run in Manchester, a schoolteacher handed in a letter at the stage door telling Crawford about an eleven-year-old leukaemia victim called Vanessa who had just had her leg amputated and was a fan of Frank Spencer. He visited the girl in hospital and arranged for her to see the show; she and her bed were transported to the nearby theatre for a matineé performance. 'I had three rows of seats removed from the circle so the bed could be fitted in,' said Crawford[1]. 'She arrived attached to a drip and attended by three nurses. That day when we performed, we all turned slightly to the left so she could see everything.'

Crawford was often at Vanessa's hospital bedside and other members of the cast sometimes turned up to entertain her and other children. One day, Crawford and the girl's father looked on as Vanessa lost her battle for life; the star, used to bringing laughter to his audiences, simply tried to make sure she died happy, concealing his tears and telling her she had just a cold and there was nothing to get upset about. 'When I told the cast she was dead, nobody spoke,' recalled Crawford[2]. 'We did the show and left the theatre in silence. We were so upset. That little girl will never leave our memories.'

Crawford put his concern for youngsters on an official level when he became president of the Sick Children's Trust, which raises money to buy homes close to hospitals so that parents who live far away can be near their seriously ill children. In October 1987 Crawford and the Duchess of York opened a home for parents of cancer victims undergoing treatment at St Bartholomew's Hospital, London.

A year later, after finishing his New York run in *The Phantom of the Opera*, Crawford was making a programme for ITV about the work of the Save the Children Fund. It came about as the result of Crawford and other stars of top British musicals making a single and album, *Save the Children*, with all the proceeds going to the charity. The stars were then asked to make a programme featuring the songs.

Crawford asked if there was anything else he could do to help, and it was suggested that he went to Africa to see the charity's work there and how funds were spent. Vaccinated against malaria, polio, cholera, hepatitis and rabies, Crawford flew to Uganda for ten days, with no intention of just looking on, but wanting to get involved with the work being carried out by the charity's volunteers.

In Uganda, Crawford found out how the Save the Children Fund was helping the people to recover from years of war and destruction. He watched as vaccines aboard his plane landing at Entebbe airport were delivered to remote communities, crucial weapons in the immunization programme that was helping to wipe out diseases such as diphtheria, whooping cough and tetanus. An immunization programme had been introduced in the Sixties but was withdrawn by the dictator Idi Amin; since its reintroduction, it had been making great strides. At one health centre, Crawford himself administered vaccine into a baby's mouth.

He went to a centre that treated undernourished children and taught parents the value of nutrition, then to an orphanage north of the capital, Kampala, in an area where half a million people had died during the years of turmoil. Joining staff who try to trace the children's surviving parents or relatives, Crawford set off in a Land Rover on a six-hour trek with a young brother and sister who knew their father had been shot dead. On one road, they came across a man who came from their village, then the children's paternal aunt. Finally, in their home village, the pair were reunited with their mother, although a joyous Crawford pointed out that many such trips end without success. He described his African tour as 'a very emotional, and very humbling, experience'[3].

Crawford was also filmed visiting a centre in Birmingham that offered playgroup facilities to pre-school children, had a toys library, an after-school club for five to ten-year-olds and an Asian women's group, and gave families the chance to enjoy holidays that they would not otherwise have. The resulting programme, *Save the Children with Michael Crawford*, mixed songs from the musical stars with film of the charity's work in Britain and Africa. It included Crawford singing 'Let's Pretend', a new song written specially by the composers of *Les Misérables*, and was screened in more than twenty countries, with profits from worldwide television sales going to the Save the Children Fund.

A lengthy introduction by the Princess Royal, President of the Save the Children Fund, started the programme. In it, she said, 'The bottom line is that, without this unique get-together and your generosity, the Save the Children Fund would not be able to provide the highly motivated and competent people who we depend on to turn our hopes for the world's children into reality for some. The success of the two records and this programme will allow the Save the Children Fund to help many more children have a brighter future.'

While appearing in Los Angeles, Crawford talked to UNICEF about becoming an 'ambassador' for the organization, something he hoped to do after making a film of *The Phantom of the Opera*. He had achieved happiness and financial security from his career; now he could give something back, travelling the world to promote the need to help starving and underprivileged children.

Chapter 20

A SPECIAL TALENT

Film producers were sending Crawford scripts at the rate of four a week while he was thrilling audiences in Los Angeles. He rejected most of them immediately, knowing that just one bad film could negate everything he had worked for over the previous twenty years. A few offers did interest him, and one day he was to be found lunching with executives of both Walt Disney Productions and Paramount Pictures. There was talk of his starring with Danny De Vito in a remake of the classic Don Quixote story.

Then there was the temptation of working in television again. In February 1990, Crawford guest-starred in Bob Hope's American television show. At the same time, the CBS network was offering him the chance to star in his own comedy series. Jeff Sagansky, newly appointed president of CBS's entertainment division, needed to pull the network up from its third position in the ratings war with the NBC and ABC networks, so he took Crawford out to lunch and offered him a team of scriptwriters who could work with him on devising a new programme.

Although tempted, Crawford decided not to rush into accepting any of these offers. Of more immediate concern to Crawford on his return to Britain in the middle of 1990 was making the film of *The Phantom of the Opera*. Andrew Lloyd Webber had already announced his intention of producing it, with Crawford and Sarah Brightman as the stars and Joel Schumacher directing. Schumacher, an American, had previously written the films *Car Wash* and *The Wiz* – a musical variation on *The Wizard of Oz*, starring Diana Ross – but had made no major box-office hits as a director. He was best known for two films aimed at the teenage market, *St Elmo's Fire* and *The Lost Boys*.

Before Crawford's return to Britain, Lloyd Webber said he had booked five sound stages, with fifty-two sets, at Pinewood Studios, west of London. A production office was set up at the studios to start planning the film, but no contracts had been signed and no stages booked[1]. When Lloyd Webber's Really Useful Group secured a distribution deal with Warner Brothers – which was also putting money into the film – the mighty American company took a three-page colour advertisement in the British film trade publication *Screen International*, saying it 'proudly announces a spectacular motion picture event for 1991' and confirming Crawford, Brightman and Schumacher's involvement[2].

The high costs of filming in Britain were blamed when Lloyd Webber subsequently pulled out of Pinewood and began looking to other parts of the world, including Eastern Europe, in the hope of reducing the budget. Some people in the film industry doubted whether the picture would ever get made; others simply thought Lloyd Webber was out of his depth in moving into films, especially with musicals, considering the low ebb they had been at in the cinema for more than a quarter of a century.

Also, two other screen productions of *Phantom* had just been made: a television movie musical, starring Charles Dance and Burt Lancaster, and a non-musical feature film, with Robert Englund and Stephanie Lawrence, who had starred in *Evita* and *Starlight Express* on stage.

In July 1990 Lloyd Webber announced that his marriage to Sarah Brightman was finished and, two months later, the film was officially shelved, although The Really Useful Group and Warner Brothers expressed their hope that the picture would eventually be made. Not a frame had been shot and Crawford unexpectedly found himself with time on his hands.

Sticking with what he knew, the star returned to the Ahmanson Theater, Los Angeles, for a special Christmas performance as the Phantom and another, short run there. Then followed his guest appearance in an American tour of *The Music of Andrew Lloyd Webber*, featuring the best-known compositions from the musical maestro's twenty years of almost unbroken success. It might not have presented Crawford with a new challenge, but it gave him the chance to continue performing while pondering what lay ahead.

Whatever the future holds, he can look back on a career that has catapulted him to fame in film, television and theatre. It is as difficult to analyse his talent as it is to unravel his complicated character. As an actor, he excels at light comedy, but he gives so much more to his performance than just acting; the stunts he insists on doing himself and the remarkable circus skills he learned for the musical *Barnum* testify to that; then there was the way he developed his singing voice for *The Phantom of the Opera*. All of this means that he cannot be judged simply as an actor.

Patsy Byrne remembers the 'little demon' who, at sixteen, impressed on stage but was 'a handful' off it, although James Roose-Evans recalls the 'shining intensity and a quality of innocence' in his performance, combined with a 'highly strung, easily depressed' personality. Melvyn Hayes will never forget the 'enthusiastic young man' who bounded on to the stage every night like the spring of a watch being released. Alan Rothwell recalls the way he mimicked the whole cast of *Two Living, One Dead*.

Bernard Braden was fooled by his 'American accent'. David Kossoff admired his instinct for knowing that 'comedy had to come up from out of the character'. Leo McKern can remember only his aura of self-importance, but Ronald Magill heard Sir Tyrone Guthrie's prediction that he would become a star. Ned Sherrin recalls sending him home in a tantrum after he protested that his fans would be mortified if he did not appear in his regular TV slot one week. Alvin Rakoff remembers teaching this 'cracking young actor' a lesson in allowing others to judge his performance. David Watkin wonders at his refusal to use a stand-in for the most dangerous of stunts.

James Cossins is happy in 'the knowledge that, were I to walk into a rehearsal room tomorrow to start work on a new show, Michael would greet me with the same affection and pleasure that always existed between us – and I expect he'd be just as bloody cheeky as well!'[4]. Claude Whatham recalls that he 'didn't have a very good reputation for being easy to work with' but ended up with his fellow-actors wanting to form a 'We Think Michael Crawford Is Marvellous Society', and Freddie Jones remembers the 'wonderful, encouraging things' he said after the two of them had shared an emotion-packed performance.

Perhaps one of the few people who has come close to understanding the Crawford psyche is film director Richard Lester, who helped him to stardom and was a close friend for several years. 'As an actor, he is technically very proficient,' says Lester[5]. 'He has a very good presence and a great physical ability to do a certain kind of work. But I think trying to make him a leading man in Hollywood at the end of the Sixties was probably a mistake. He is quite special, and maybe that's one of his problems. He really needs material that's absolutely tailored to his talent. My overall memory of Michael is that "Take 2" of him coming up out of the water in his tweed jacket, on water skis, when all the professionals said: "That's technically impossible." That's Michael. He's unique.'

As Crawford looks for new challenges in the Nineties, his position as an internationally acclaimed entertainer is undisputed; his reputation as a workaholic and perfectionist is legendary. Behind the mask lies the flipside, partly the price of success, partly a reflection of his emotional, sensitive character: the 'father' who never was, the stepfather he hated, the 'secret' daughter, the wife who lost out when it came to a choice between work and marriage. As Crawford once said, 'In the theatre, I give my life to people. Whether there's much left over must remain a moot point.'[6]

NOTES

1 The Little Sweep

1 Marriage certificate obtained from the Registrar General of Births, Deaths & Marriages, London.

2 Letter to the author from the Ministry of Defence Air Historical Branch, dated 27 March 1990 (confirmed by a subsequent letter, dated 12 April 1990); Royal Air Force Operations Record Book for 66 Squadron, held at the Public Record Office, Kew, Surrey; death certificate obtained from the Registrar General of Births, Deaths & Marriages, London.

3 Birth certificate obtained from the Registrar General of Births, Deaths & Marriages.

4 *The Battle of Britain Then and Now*, ed. Winston G. Ramsey (Battle of Britain Prints International Ltd, 1980); *Fighter Squadrons of the RAF and Their Aircraft*, John D. R. Rawlings (Macdonald & Co, 1969). Duxford, near Cambridge, where Sgt Smith was based, was the RAF's first Spitfire station; both 66 and 19 Squadrons were fully equipped with Spitfires.

5 Royal Air Force Operations Record Book for 66 Squadron, held at the Public Record Office, Kew, Surrey; *Fighter Squadrons of the RAF and Their Aircraft*, John D. R. Rawlings (Macdonald & Co., 1969).

6 *The Battle of Britain Then and Now*, ed. Winston G. Ramsey (Battle of Britain Prints International Ltd, 1980); *Battle of Britain*, Len Deighton and Max Hastings (Michael Joseph, 1990). Flying Officer Douglas Bader was posted to 19 Squadron, then 222 Squadron as flight commander, then took charge of 242 Squadron, before taking command of the Duxford Wing in August 1940.

7 Royal Air Force Operations Record Book for 66 Squadron, held at the Public Record Office, Kew, Surrey.

8 ibid.

9 Royal Air Force Operations Record Book for 66 Squadron, held at the Public Record Office, Kew, Surrey; *The Battle of Britain Then and Now*,

ed. Winston G. Ramsey (Battle of Britain Prints International Ltd, 1980); *Sheerness Times & Guardian* (2 August 1940 and 13 September 1940).

10 Reported in the *Sheerness Times & Guardian* (2 August 1940 and 13 September 1940).

11 Letter to the author from the Ministry of Defence Air Historical Branch, dated 27 March 1990 (a further letter, dated 12 April 1990, pointed out that all information contained in the previous letter was confirmed by the RAF Personnel Management Centre and the Commonwealth War Graves Commission); Royal Air Force Operations Record Book for 66 Squadron, held at the Public Record Office, Kew, Surrey; *The Battle of Britain Then and Now*, ed. Winston G. Ramsey (Battle of Britain Prints International Ltd, 1980); *RAF Kenley*, Peter Flint (Terence Dalton Ltd, 1985); reported in the *Sheerness Times & Guardian* (13 September 1940), *Kent Messenger* (14 September 1940), *Kentish Express* (20 September 1940).

12 I am indebted to Denis Bishop of Mersham, Kent, for help and advice with local research.

13 Letters to the author from the Ministry of Defence Air Historical Branch, dated 27 March and 12 April 1990; Royal Air Force Operations Record Book for 66 Squadron, held at the Public Record Office, Kew, Surrey; *The Battle of Britain Then and Now*, ed. Winston G. Ramsey (Battle of Britain Prints International Ltd. 1980).

14 Letters to the author from the Ministry of Defence Air Historical Branch, dated 27 March and 12 April 1990; the parish register of funerals conducted at the church includes his full name, Arthur Dumbell Smith. I am grateful to the Rev. John Smith, vicar of St Luke's Church, Whyteleafe, Surrey, for making available the parish register and the 'Roll of Honour to Commemorate the Pilots Who Flew From RAF Kenley During the Battle of Britain'.

15 The RAF number on Sgt Smith's gravestone matches that included on his certificate of marriage to Doris Agnes Mary Pike.

16 *Sheerness Times & Guardian* (13 September 1940).

17 Address given on birth certificate, obtained from the Registrar General of Births, Deaths & Marriages, London.

18 *Plain Soldiering: A History of the Armed Forces on Salisbury Plain*, N. D. G. James (The Hobnob Press, 1987).

19 Birth certificate obtained from the Registrar General of Births, Deaths & Marriages, London. The certificate recorded the name of his mother as Doris Agnes Mary Smith, formerly Pike, but did not record the father's name or occupation.

20 *Plain Soldiering: A History of the Armed Forces on Salisbury Plain*, N. D. G. James (The Hobnob Press, 1987).

21 Marriage certificate obtained from the Registrar General of Births, Deaths & Marriages, London. The certificate recorded the marriage of Lionel Dennis Ingram, twenty-eight, bachelor, to Doris Agnes Mary Smith, twenty-seven, widow.

22 *Petticoat* (24 August 1974).

23 *Time* (2 June 1967).

24 ibid.

25 *Woman's Own* (9 March 1985).

26 *Woman's Own* (9 March 1985) and the *Sunday Express Magazine* (17 January 1988).

27 A year later, the annual Aldeburgh Festival was founded, in the Suffolk coastal town to which Britten had moved, and he used it as a showcase for his new works. The English Opera Group was later succeeded by the English Music Theatre Company. Benjamin Britten died on 4 December 1976.

28 *Let's Make an Opera* was written and originally performed in 1949. Its first half is a play in which children and adults plan their production together, and the second half is the musical work itself, *The Little Sweep*.

29 *Woman* (25 May 1974).

30 Colin Graham interviewed by the author (9 July 1990).

31 *The Little Beggars*, loosely based on *The Beggar's Opera*, John Gay's satirical play about the eighteenth-century fashion for Italian opera and about Prime Minister Sir Robert Walpole, was later made as a television production, but Michael Crawford and David Hemmings were then too old for their child roles. The radio version was a BBC nomination for the Italia Prize.

32 *A Small Thing – Like an Earthquake*, Ned Sherrin (autobiography), (Weidenfeld & Nicolson, 1983).

33 *Petticoat* (24 August 1974).

2 Taking the Biscuit

1 *Monthly Film Bulletin* (February 1958).

2 *Monthly Film Bulletin* (December 1958).

3 *Noye's Fludde* received its première on 18 June 1958 and was performed at Orford Church again on 19 and 21 June.

4 Reported in the *East Anglian Daily Times* (21 June 1958).

5 *East Anglian Daily Times* (19 June 1958).

6 Colin Graham interviewed by the author (9 July 1990).

7 *Coventry Evening Telegraph* (5 September 1958).

8 Patsy Byrne interviewed by the author (2 June 1990).

9 Letter from James Roose-Evans to the author, dated 27 July 1990.

10 *Coventry Evening Telegraph* (2 September 1958).

11 *Birmingham Post* (2 September 1958).

12 I am grateful to *Oxford Mail* theatre critic Don Chapman for research assistance on the Belgrade Theatre production of *Head of the Family* in Oxford.

13 The New York Drama Critics' Circle had already named John Osborne's *Look Back in Anger* the best foreign play of 1958. *Epitaph for George Dillon*, about the position of the artist in contemporary society, failed to attract audiences.

14 *The Stage* (1 January 1959).
15 *Stratford Herald* (2 January 1959).

3 Waiting for a Break

1 Crawford was in crowd scenes for this schoolboy series, which ran on BBC television between 1952 and 1962. He was in one series.
2 Crawford played a schoolboy footballer in *Probation Officer*.
3 Melvyn Hayes interviewed by the author (2 June 1990).
4 In 1962 Kops said that he and his contemporaries John Arden, Robert Bolt, Willis Hall, Alun Owen and Arnold Wesker would ensure this.
5 *Manchester Guardian* (3 March 1960).
6 Sonnie Hale (Robert Hale Munro) made his name as a British stage star in the Twenties and later appeared in films. He also directed two 1937 film musicals starring Jessie Matthews, *Head Over Heels* and *Gangway*.
7 Jeremy Bulloch interviewed by the author (14 June 1990).
8 Artists' Contracts, *Two Living, One Dead*, Item 22 of the Teddy Baird Collection, held at the British Film Institute.
9 Gunnar Fischer had been cameraman on most of Swedish director Ingmar Bergman's films.
10 Alan Rothwell interviewed by the author (30 June 1990).
11 *Two Living, One Dead* received its world première in Oslo, Norway, on 16 March 1961.
12 *Dagens Nyheter* (5 April 1961).
13 *Morgenbladet*, Oslo (17 March 1961).
14 The first series of *Danger Man* was broadcast in America during 1961. Two later series were broadcast in America under a different title, *Secret Agent*, in 1965 and 1966.
15 In America the series was called *The Adventures of Sir Francis Drake* and was broadcast during 1962, as a summer replacement for the comedy series *Car 54, Where Are You?*
16 Peter Graham Scott's award-winning production of *The Quare Fellow* was a TV version of the Brendan Behan 1954 stage play set in a prison on the eve of an execution, which helped to change some people's attitudes to capital punishment.
17 Peter Graham Scott interviewed by the author (25 July 1990).
18 Letter to the author from Terence Morgan, dated 27 August 1990.
19 Confirmed by ITC Entertainment, the programme's distributor, 30 July 1990.
20 Steve McQueen made the film only because it brought him to Britain, where he could indulge his passion for motor racing, according to *Steve McQueen – The Unauthorized Biography*, Malachy McCoy (New American Library, 1975).
21 *Nineteen* (June 1973).
22 *The Daily Cinema* (28 May 1963).

23 *The Film Greats*, Barry Norman (Hodder and Stoughton/British Broad-casting Corporation, 1985).
24 ibid.
25 *McQueen: The Untold Story of a Bad Boy In Hollywood*, Penina Spiegel (Berkley Books, New York, 1987).
26 Chuck Julian interviewed by the author (21 June 1990).
27 ibid.

4 Blowing his Horn

1 *Sergeant Bilko* was the title used for syndication of *The Phil Silvers Show*, which was broadcast by CBS in America. The programme began in 1955 as *You'll Never Get Rich* and, in less than two months, it changed its title to *The Phil Silvers Show*.
2 Bernard Braden interviewed by the author (4 July 1990).
3 David Kossoff interviewed by the author (12 June 1990).
4 *Daily Mail* (28 February 1962).
5 *The Daily Telegraph* (28 February 1962).
6 *Time* (2 June 1967).
7 *Radio Times* (30 September 1971).
8 *Daily Telegraph* (14 May 1965).
9 Death certificate obtained from the Registrar General of Births, Deaths & Marriages, London.
10 London *Evening News* (20 February 1974).
11 Press release issued at the time of *The Jokers* film release, 1967.
12 *Nottingham Evening Post* (14 December 1963).
13 *Financial Times* (13 December 1963).
14 *Daily Telegraph* (19 December 1963).
15 Ronald Magill joined the ITV serial *Emmerdale Farm* when it began, in 1972. The programme shortened its title to *Emmerdale* in 1989. Ronald Magill left in 1990.
16 Ronald Magill interviewed by the author (6 June 1990).
17 Ken McReddie interviewed by the author (21 June 1990).
18 Letter from Leo McKern to the author, dated 28 June 1990.
19 *Daily Express* (3 February 1983).
20 *Radio Times* (21 December 1974–3 January 1975).
21 Colin Graham interviewed by the author (9 July 1990).
22 *The Times* (9 July 1964).
23 Stephen Moore interviewed by the author (21 June 1990).

5 The Knack/Byron

1 *Radio Times* (30 September 1971).
2 ibid.
3 Richard Lester interviewed by the author (3 July 1990).
4 ibid.
5 ibid.

6 *Richard Lester: A Guide to References and Resources*, Diane Rosenfeldt (George Prior Publishers, London, and GIC Hall & Co, Boston, Massachusetts, 1978).
7 David Watkin interviewed by the author (10 June 1990).
8 Richard Lester interviewed by the author (3 July 1990).
9 *Radio Times* (30 September 1971).
10 *Films and Filming* (July 1965).
11 *Daily Worker* (1 June 1965).
12 *Sunday Express* (6 June 1965).
13 Alec McCowen starred in the subsequent television version of *The Little Beggars*.
14 *A Small Thing – Like an Earthquake*, Ned Sherrin (autobiography), (Weidenfeld & Nicolson, 1983).
15 Ned Sherrin interviewed by the author (20 June 1990).
16 Peter Dobereiner interviewed by the author (30 June 1990).
17 *Nineteen* (June 1973).
18 *A Small Thing – Like an Earthquake*, Ned Sherrin (autobiography), (Weidenfeld & Nicolson, 1983).
19 ibid.
20 *Nineteen* (June 1973).
21 London *Evening Standard* (2 September 1964).
22 *Daily Mail* (2 September 1964).
23 Harry H. Corbett's classical theatre performances included *Richard II, Hamlet* and *Macbeth*.
24 Harry H. Corbett played Harold Steptoe, son of Albert, played by Wilfrid Brambell.
25 *Sunday Express* (11 April 1965).
26 London *Evening Standard* (9 April 1965).
27 The original stage production of *A Funny Thing Happened On the Way To the Forum* opened at the Alvin Theater, New York, on 8 May 1962.
28 Richard Lester interviewed by the author (3 July 1990)
29 ibid.
30 ibid.
31 *Variety* (28 September 1966).

6 Families

1 *The Observer Magazine* (31 January 1988).
2 Marriage certificate obtained from the Registrar General of Births, Deaths & Marriages, London.
3 Birth certificate obtained from the Registrar General of Births, Deaths & Marriages, London.
4 Birth certificate obtained from the Registrar General of Births, Deaths & Marriages, London.
5 *The Sun* (12 December 1964).
6 *Woman* (21 May 1988).

7 Richard Lester interviewed by the author (3 July 1990).
8 ibid.
9 Cited in *Do You Sleep In the Nude?*, Rex Reed (New American Library, New York, 1968).
10 Marriage certificate obtained from the Registrar General of Births, Deaths & Marriages, London.
11 *The Sun* (27 December 1973).
12 A former chauffeur of Michael Crawford claimed in a newspaper in 1981 that the star had once told him he paid £4,000.

7 Black Comedies

1 Letter to the author from James Cossins, dated 3 June 1990.
2 *The Times* (21 April 1966).
3 *Punch* (27 April 1966).
4 *The Sunday Times* (24 April 1966).
5 Letter to the author from James Cossins, dated 3 June 1990.
6 Cited in *The Films of Michael Winner*, Bill Harding (Frederick Muller Ltd, London, 1978).
7 *London Life* (10 September 1966).
8 ibid.
9 ibid.
10 ibid.
11 Oliver Reed interviewed by the author (26 June 1990).
12 ibid.
13 ibid.
14 *The Hollywood Reporter* (25 April 1967).
15 *Time* (19 April 1967).
16 London *Evening Standard* (15 June 1967).
17 Alvin Rakoff interviewed by the author (29 June 1990).
18 Richard Lester interviewed by the author (3 July 1990).
19 Letter to the author from James Cossins, dated 3 June 1990.
20 *Do You Sleep In the Nude?*, Rex Reed (New American Library, New York, 1968).
21 David Watkin interviewed by the author (10 June 1990).
22 *Nineteen* (June 1973).
23 *The Observer* (22 October 1967).
24 *Variety* (25 October 1967).
25 *Films In Review* (June–July 1967).
26 *Film Quarterly* (Winter 1967–68).
27 Richard Lester interviewed by the author (3 July 1990).
28 *The Sun* (24 October 1967).
29 ibid.
30 London *Evening News* (27 October 1967).
31 Cited in *Do You Sleep In the Nude?*, Rex Reed (New American Library, New York, 1968).

32 ibid.
33 London *Evening News* (27 July 1970).
34 *Time* (2 June 1967).
35 *The New York Times* (13 February 1967).
36 *Newsweek* (20 February 1967).
37 *Sunday Express* (17 May 1987).
38 *Do You Sleep In the Nude?*, Rex Reed (New American Library, New York, 1968).
39 ibid.

8 Hello, Dolly!

1 *Photoplay* (May 1969).
2 *Sunday Mirror* (11 August 1968).
3 *Photoplay* (May 1969).
4 *Gene Kelly*, Clive Hirschhorn (W. H. Allen, 1984).
5 *Action* (March–April 1969).
6 *Petticoat* (13 February 1967).
7 *Sunday Express* (17 May 1987).
8 ibid.
9 *Gene Kelly*, Clive Hirschhorn (W. H. Allen, 1984).
10 ibid.
11 *Photoplay* (May 1969).
12 *Gene Kelly*, Clive Hirschhorn (W. H. Allen, 1984).
13 ibid.
14 London *Evening Standard* (25 April 1975).
15 *Petticoat* (13 February 1967).
16 *Variety* (24 December 1969).
17 *Motion Picture Herald* (7 January 1970).
18 *The Hollywood Reporter* (18 December 1969).
19 *Today's Cinema* (2 January 1970).
20 *Kinematograph Weekly* (27 December 1969).
21 *Films and Filming* (February 1970).
22 *Daily Mirror* (23 December 1969).
23 *Barbra*, Donald Zec and Anthony Fowles (New English Library, 1981).

9 Games People Play

1 *The Observer* (23 February 1969).
2 *Daily Sketch* (20 March 1969).
3 Cited in *Photoplay* (July 1969).
4 ibid.
5 *The Films of Michael Winner*, Bill Harding (Frederick Muller Ltd, London, 1978).
6 *Today's Cinema* (26 June 1970).

7 *Variety* (8 April 1970).
8 *Films and Filming* (July 1970).
9 *Record & Radio Mirror* (8 June 1974).
10 Ronald Neame interviewed by the author (28 June 1990).
11 London *Evening News* (25 August 1969).
12 ibid.
13 *Daily Mail* (19 November 1971).
14 *The Times* (30 October 1970).
15 *Kinematograph Weekly* (15 August 1970).
16 *Motion Picture Herald* (29 July 1970).
17 *The Sun* (24 December 1970).
18 *Woman* (16 October 1971).
19 *Daily Mail* (19 November 1971).
20 *Woman's Own* (12 January 1974).
21 *Daily Mail* (19 November 1971).
22 London *Evening Standard* (8 July 1971).

10 No Sex, Please

1 *Daily Mail* (19 November 1971).
2 London *Evening News* (4 June 1971).
3 Robert Hirsch was a French character actor of the *Comédie Française*.
4 *The Times* (4 June 1971).
5 *Daily Telegraph* (4 June 1971).
6 London *Evening Standard* (8 July 1971).
7 ibid.
8 London *Evening Standard* (17 August 1972).
9 *Alice In Wonderland* was made by Walt Disney in 1951. Other film productions include a 1933 American live-action version featuring stars such as Gary Cooper, W. C. Fields and Cary Grant in masks, a 1950 British version mixing live action and puppets, and a 1950 French puppet version.
10 Publicity material issued at the time of *Alice's Adventures in Wonderland* film release.
11 *The Hollywood Reporter* (12 June 1972).
12 *Variety* (15 November 1972).
13 *Films and Filming* (May 1973).
14 *CinemaTV Today* (9 December 1972).
15 *Monthly Film Bulletin* (January 1973).
16 *Woman's Own* (12 January 1974).
17 *Daily Express* (14 January 1974).
18 *Sunday Express* (17 May 1987).
19 *Daily Mail* (31 October 1975).
20 *Sunday Express* (17 May 1987).
21 ibid.

11 Some Mothers

1 Raymond Allen interviewed by the author (3 August 1990).
2 ibid.
3 ibid.
4 ibid.
5 *Daily Mail* (21 December 1973).
6 ibid.
7 London *Evening Standard* (19 December 1973).
8 *Sunday People* (26 August 1973).
9 *Daily Mirror* (28 February 1973).
10 Derek Ware interviewed by the author (13 July 1990).
11 ibid.
12 *Daily Mail* (22 February 1973).
13 *Daily Mirror* (16 February 1973).
14 *Daily Mail* (16 March 1973).
15 Raymond Allen interviewed by the author (3 August 1990).
16 Gavin Birkett interviewed by the author (3 August 1990).
17 ibid.
18 Stuart Fell interviewed by the author (31 July 1990).
19 ibid.
20 James Cossins interviewed by the author (29 May 1990).
21 ibid.
22 Marc Boyle interviewed by the author (1 August 1990).
23 *Daily Mirror* (20 December 1973).
24 *Daily Mirror* (21 December 1973).
25 *TVTimes* (6 June 1974).
26 *Radio Times* (15 November 1973).
27 *Woman* (9 February 1974).
28 Gavin Birkett interviewed by the author (3 August 1990).
29 Stuart Fell interviewed by the author (31 July 1990).
30 Gavin Birkett interviewed by the author (3 August 1990).

12 Billy

1 *Sunday Telegraph* (28 April 1974).
2 *The Guardian* (1 May 1974).
3 *Petticoat* (24 August 1974).
4 *Daily Mirror* (23 April 1974).
5 *Woman* (25 May 1974).
6 London *Evening News* (2 May 1974).
7 *Daily Express* (2 May 1974).
8 *Daily Mail* (2 May 1974).
9 British song-and-dance actor Jack Buchanan was a stage star of the Twenties and made many films up until his death in 1957. He was one of the first actors to play Bulldog Drummond on screen, in the 1925 silent film *Bulldog Drummond's Third Round*.

10 *The Tatler* (June 1974).
11 *Observer Magazine* (31 January 1988).
12 *News of the World* (28 December 1975).
13 Cited in the *Daily Mail* (29 November 1975).
14 Roy Castle interviewed by the author (15 July 1990).

13 Same Time, Different Actress

1 London *Evening Standard* (17 September 1976).
2 *Daily Mail* (24 September 1976).
3 *Daily Telegraph* (24 September 1976).
4 *Daily Express* (24 September 1976).
5 *Daily Express* (15 January 1977).
6 *Sunday People* (16 January 1977).
7 ibid.
8 London *Evening News* (8 September 1977).
9 *Sunday People* (16 January 1977).
10 *Daily Express* (12 January 1977).

14 Grandmothers, Dissidents and Mothers Again

1 *The Sun* (8 November 1978).
2 *The Sun* (19 August 1985).
3 Innes Lloyd interviewed by the author (7 July 1990).
4 Claude Whatham interviewed by the author (24 July 1990).
5 ibid.
6 Freddie Jones interviewed by the author (15 July 1990).
7 Claude Whatham interviewed by the author (24 July 1990).
8 ibid.
9 Freddie Jones interviewed by the author (15 July 1990).
10 Claude Whatham interviewed by the author (24 July 1990).
11 Freddie Jones interviewed by the author (15 July 1990).
12 Claude Whatham interviewed by the author (24 July 1990).
13 Freddie Jones interviewed by the author (15 July 1990).
14 Claude Whatham interviewed by the author (24 July 1990).
15 *The Listener* (30 November 1978).
16 ibid.
17 *The Times* (22 November 1978).
18 Cited in *The Guardian* (11 December 1989).
19 The top three programmes, in order, were *Some Mothers Do 'Ave 'Em, All Creatures Great and Small* and *Larry Grayson's Generation Game. Bruce Forsyth's Big Night*, which was broadcast over several hours on ITV, did not make the Top 20 chart. Forsyth had previously presented *The Generation Game* on the BBC and, in 1990, he returned to make a new series, *Bruce Forsyth's Generation Game*.

20 *Radio Times* (11 November 1972).
21 *The Observer* (19 November 1978).
22 Raymond Allen interviewed by the author (3 August 1990).
23 Val Musetti interviewed by the author (29 July 1990).
24 ibid.
25 Rick Gauld interviewed by the author (15 July 1990).
26 Raymond Allen interviewed by the author (3 August 1990).

15 Fathers, Flowers and Fantasies

1 *Sunday Express* (6 May 1979).
2 *Daily Mail* (31 March 1979).
3 *Daily Express* (3 April 1979).
4 London *Evening News* (3 April 1979).
5 *Daily Mail* (3 April 1979).
6 *The Sun* (2 June 1979).
7 *Financial Times* (15 June 1979).
8 *Sunday Mirror* (1 July 1979).
9 *Daily Mail* (22 April 1980).
10 Marc Boyle interviewed by the author (1 August 1990).
11 *Sunday Mirror* (15 February 1981).
12 Charles Jarrott interviewed by the author (13 August 1990).
13 ibid.
14 *The Hollywood Reporter* (5 August 1980).
15 Oliver Reed interviewed by the author (26 June 1990).
16 *Daily Mail* (3 July 1981).
17 *Variety* (5 August 1981).

16 Barnum

1 *The South Bank Show*, broadcast on ITV, 31 March 1985.
2 ibid.
3 *Daily Mail* and *Daily Express* (2 June 1981).
4 *Sunday Express* (7 March 1982).
5 Cited in *The Guinness Book of Theatre Facts & Feats*, Michael Billington (Guinness Superlatives, 1982).
6 ibid.
7 *The New Standard*, London (12 June 1981).
8 Cited in the *Daily Mail* (26 June 1981).
9 *Daily Mirror* (13 June 1981).
10 *Financial Times* (12 June 1981).
11 *Punch* (June 1981).
12 Cited in *The Sunday Times Magazine* (11 October 1987).
13 Alan Benson interviewed by the author (27 July 1990).
14 ibid.

15 *Daily Express* (2 March 1985).
16 Death certificate obtained from the Registrar General of Births, Deaths & Marriages, London. Edith Pike had married twice and had nine children.
17 *Sunday* (3 March 1985).

17 The Phantom

1 Director Brian De Palma subsequently cast Sissy Spacek in the lead role in the 1976 American film *Carrie*. She had already starred in the 1973 film *Badlands*.
2 Tim Rice wrote the words for *Chess*, and former Abba composers and performers Benny Andersson and Bjorn Ulvaeus wrote the music.
3 *Daily Mail* (11 October 1986).
4 No other original-cast musical album had ever gone straight to No. 1 in the charts.
5 *The Times* (10 October 1986).
6 *Daily Telegraph* (11 October 1986).
7 *Financial Times* (10 October 1986).
8 Cited in the *Daily Express* (21 October 1986).
9 Cited in the *Daily Mail* (11 October 1986).
10 Colin Graham interviewed by the author (9 July 1990).
11 Two years later, Crawford released another album, *With Love*, accompanied by the London Symphony Orchestra. It was a mixture of pop songs and musical hits. A new version of 'The Music of the Night', from *The Phantom of the Opera*, was proof of how Crawford's voice had developed and gained strength since the show's opening.
12 Colin Graham interviewed by the author (9 July 1990).
13 Colm Wilkinson subsequently starred in the Canadian production of *The Phantom of the Opera*. He was, in fact, Andrew Lloyd Webber's first Phantom, performing the role at the Sydmonton Festival, an annual event at the composer's country home, during the musical's embryonic stages.

18 Phantom Takes Flight

1 In late 1990, it looked as if *Miss Saigon*, another British stage musical, from the creators of *Les Misérables*, would break this record by the time it opened on Broadway in 1991.
2 *The New York Times* (27 January 1988).
3 *USA Today* (27 January 1988).
4 *The New York Times* (28 January 1988).
5 *The New York Times* (14 February 1988).
6 *Newsweek* (8 February 1988).
7 *Sunday Express* (31 January 1988).
8 *Woman* (21 May 1988).
9 *Sunday Mirror* (24 April 1988).

10 Birth certificate obtained from the Registrar General of Births, Deaths & Marriages, London.
11 *Los Angeles Times* (2 June 1989).
12 *The Sun* (26 July 1989).

19 Saving the Children

1 *TVTimes* (17 December 1988–1 January 1989).
2 *Sunday Mirror* (21 December 1986).
3 *Sunday Mirror* (11 December 1988).

20 A Special Talent

1 Confirmed by Pinewood Studios (31 July 1990).
2 *Screen International* (19–25 May 1990).
3 Cited in *The Sunday Times* (10 June 1990).
4 Letter to the author from James Cossins, dated 3 June 1990.
5 Richard Lester interviewed by the author (3 July 1990).
6 Cited in *You* magazine (12 October 1988).

APPENDIX A

Theatre

Let's Make an Opera (Scala Theatre, London, followed by British tour and Royal Court Theatre, London, 1955), Sam the Little Sweep/Gay Brook.

Noye's Fludde (Orford Church, Suffolk, during Aldeburgh Festival, and Southwark Cathedral, London, 1958), Jaffet.

Head of the Family (Belgrade Theatre, Coventry, and Oxford Playhouse, 1958), André Dulac.

Out of the Frying Plan (Belgrade Theatre, Coventry, 1958–9), Nuri.

Julius Caesar (Belgrade Theatre, Coventry, 1959) Lucius.

Change for the Angel (Arts Theatre Club, London, 1960), Martin Jenkins.

Come Blow Your Horn (Prince of Wales Theatre, London, 1962–3), Buddy Baker.

Coriolanus (Nottingham Playhouse, 1963–4), Second Citizen and Second Servingman.

The Importance of Being Earnest (Nottingham Playhouse, 1963–4), Algernon Moncrieff.

March Hares (British tour, 1964), Glaydon.

Twelfth Night (New Shakespeare Company tour of Britain and Portugal, 1964), Feste.

The Striplings (New Arts Theatre Club, London, 1964), Biff.

Travelling Light (Prince of Wales Theatre, London, 1965), Arnold Champion.

The Anniversary (Duke of York's Theatre, London, 1966), Tom.

Black Comedy/White Lies (Boston, 1967; Ethel Barrymore Theater, New York, 1967), Brindsley Miller/Tom.

No Sex, Please – We're British (British tour, opening in Edinburgh, 1971; Strand Theatre, London, 1971–2), Brian Runnicles.

Billy (Palace Theatre, Manchester, 1974; Theatre Royal, Drury Lane, London, 1974–6), Billy Fisher.

Royal Variety Performance: Excerpts from *Billy* (London Palladium, 1975), Billy Fisher.

Same Time, Next Year (Theatre Royal, Norwich, 1976; Prince of Wales Theatre, London, 1976–7), George.

Flowers for Algernon (Queen's Theatre, London, 1979), Charlie Gordon.

Barnum (London Palladium, 1981–3; Opera House, Manchester, 1984–5; Victoria Palace, London, 1985–6), Phineas Taylor Barnum.

The Phantom of the Opera (Her Majesty's Theatre, London, 1986–7; Majestic Theater, New York, 1988; Ahmanson Theater, Los Angeles, 1989–90). The Phantom of the Opera.

APPENDIX B

APPENDIX C

Television

Billy Bunter (BBC, one series, 1959).

Probation Officer (ITV, one episode, 1960), John.

Emergency – Ward 10 (ITV, one episode, 1960), Brian Kennedy.

The Chequered Flag (ITV, three episodes in six-part series, 1960), Bryan West.

The Guinea Pig (ITV, play, 1960), George Read.

Police Surgeon (ITV, one episode).

The Siege of Kilfaddy (BBC, play).

The Seekers (BBC, play).

Sir Francis Drake (ITV, series, 1961–2; broadcast in America by NBC as *The Adventures of Sir Francis Drake*, 1962), John Drake.

Destiny (BBC, play, 1962).

Still Life (CBC, Canada, play, 1963).

Not So Much a Programme, More a Way of Life (BBC, series, 1964–5), Byron.

The Move After Checkmate (ITV, *Play of the Week*, 1966), Tony Sellman.

The Three Barrelled Shotgun (ITV, *Armchair Theatre*, 1966), Edward.

The Policeman and the Cook (ITV, play, 1970), Constable Gough.

Quiz Ball (BBC1, guest in one episode, 1972).

Some Mothers Do 'Ave 'Em (BBC1, first series of seven, and second series of six episodes, 1973, Christmas specials 1974 and 1975), Frank Spencer.

What's My Line? (BBC1, guest, 1973).

Parkinson (BBC1, guest interviewee, 1976).

To Be Perfectly Frank (BBC1, 1977). Behind-the-scenes look at stunts for *Some Mothers Do 'Ave 'Em*.

Some Mothers Do 'Ave 'Em (BBC1, third series of seven episodes, 1978), Frank Spencer.

Play for Today: Sorry … (Private View/Audience) (BBC1, double-bill, 1978), Ferdinand Vanek.

Chalk and Cheese (ITV, series of six episodes, 1979), Dave Finn.

Multi-Coloured Swap Shop (BBC1, guest appearance, 1981).

Film 81 (BBC1, guest interviewee, 1981).

The Electric Theatre Show (ITV, guest interviewee, 1981).
Weekend Special: Tribute to Michael Crawford (Granada TV, 1985).
The South Bank Show (ITV, subject of half-hour film, 1985).
Barnum (BBC1, TV film version of stage show, 1986) Phineas Taylor Barnum.
Going Live! (BBC1, guest appearance, 1987).
Save the Children with Michael Crawford (ITV, presenter, 1988).
The Bob Hope Show (US TV, guest, 1990).

APPENDIX D

Records

Albums

The Little Sweep
The Knack ... and how to get it
A Funny Thing Happened On the Way To the Forum
Hello, Dolly!
The Games
Billy
Flowers for Algernon (USA only)
Barnum
The Phantom of the Opera
Songs From the Stage and Screen (with the London Symphony Orchestra)
With Love (with the London Symphony Orchestra)

Singles

Walking Round
The Knack (title song from the film)
Lady From LA/I Missed the Last Rainbow (from *Billy*)
Disney Girls/True Love Ways
The Music of the Night (from *The Phantom of the Opera*)

INDEX

Index

Baker, Hylda 13
Baker, Stanley 64
Bakewell, Joan 112
Baldwin, Harry 78, 153
Baldwin, Pauline 77
Baldwin, Sam 78, 153
Baldwin, Tommy 77, 78, 153
Bannen, Ian 16
Bar Mitzvah Boy 97
Barber, John 73, 103, 141
Barbra (biography of Barbra
    Streisand) 61–2
Barker, Ronnie 132
Barnum (musical) 1, 78, 126–35,
    136, 139, 155, 158, 163
    reviews of 130–32
Barnum, Phineas Taylor 126
Barry, John 75, 95
Bartman, Frederick 13, 27
Barton, Steve 144, 145, 147
BBC
Beatles, The 29, 48, 49
Bedford General Hospital 134
Beeny, Christopher 16
Beere, Christopher 131
Belgrade Theatre Coventry 10, 11,
    12, 13
Bennett, Robert Russell 150
Benson 156
Benson, Alan 133–4
Bentley, Dick 116
Berlin Philharmonic Orchestra 154
Bertram Mills' Circus 1
Bilbow, Marjorie 61, 65, 76
Billy (musical) 78, 93, 95–101, 102,
    128, 158
    reviews of 98–100
Billy Bunter (TV) 14, 16
Billy Liar 95, 99
Binder, Paul 126
Birabeau, André 11, 12
Birkett, Gavin 86, 87, 93
Birkin, Jane 153
Birmingham Post 12
Björnson, Maria 148, 149, 154
Black, Don 75, 95, 98
Black, Isobel 19
Black, Peter 85
Black Comedy (play) 46, 51–4, 55,
    147 (see also *White Lies*)
    reviews of 53

Blair, Lionel 98
Bloom, Claire 98
Blow Your Own Trumpet (film) 9
    review of 9
Bogart, Humphrey
Bolcom, William 151
Boone, Pat 6
Booth, Shirley 56
Boulting Brothers 16
Bowles, Peter 96, 97
Bowman, Andy 83
Boyle, Billy 97
Boyle, Marc 89, 93, 122
Braden, Bernard 22, 163
Bragg, Melvyn 133
Brahms, Caryl 7, 33
Bramble, Mark 130
Bridge, Andrew 149, 154
Brief Lives 95
Briers, Richard 12
Brigadoon 139
Brightman, Sarah 136–7, 138, 139,
    140, 142, 143, 144, 145, 146,
    147, 148, 150, 152, 162
British Amateur Gymnastics
    Association 134
British Lion 23
Britten, Benjamin 5, 6, 10, 23, 140,
    146
Brixton Town Hall 5
Broadway 12, 22, 46, 51, 53, 54,
    55, 57, 60, 69, 98, 102, 104,
    105, 108, 126, 129, 130, 131,
    132, 146, 147, 148, 154, 155,
    156
Bron, Eleanor 33
Bronston Studios, Madrid 37
Brooks, Ray 29, 74
Brothers In Law 16
Browning Version, The 17
Bruce Forsyth's Big Night 113
Bryant, Margot 92
Buchanan, Jack 100
Buckingham Palace 145
Bulford Army camp 4
Bulloch, Jeremy 16–17
Bunnage, Avis 96, 99
Burstyn, Ellen 102
Bushey Studios 8
Butterworth, Peter 9
Byrne, Patsy 11, 163